Faith &
Freedom

Faith & Freedom

The Founding Fathers in Their Own Words

Robert Gingrich

BARBOUR
PUBLISHING

Published by Barbour Publishing, Inc., P.O. Box 719, Uhrichsville,
Ohio 44683, www.barbourbooks.com

*Our mission is to publish and distribute inspirational products offering
exceptional value and biblical encouragement to the masses.*

Member of the
Evangelical Christian
Publishers Association

Printed in the United States of America.

Contents

Introduction

This book is intended as a reminder to twenty-first-century Americans that most of the men we recognize as our nation's Founding Fathers were exceptional people who were guided by their Christian faith in establishing the foundation upon which the United States of America became the most powerful and prosperous nation the world has ever known.

Regarding the importance of understanding our history, Supreme Court Justice Joseph Story wrote in his *Commentaries on the Constitution* (1833):

> *Let the American youth never forget,*
> *that they possess a noble inheritance,*
> *bought by the toils and sufferings and*
> *blood of their ancestors; and capacity,*
> *if wisely improved, and faithfully*
> *guarded, of transmitting to their latest*
> *posterity all the substantial blessings of*
> *life, the peaceful enjoyment of liberty,*
> *property, religion, and independence.*
> *The structure has been erected by*
> *architects of consummate skill and*
> *fidelity; its foundations are solid; its*
> *compartments are beautiful, as well*
> *as useful; its arrangements are full of*

> *wisdom and order; and its defenses are*
> *impregnable from without. It has been*
> *reared for immortality, if the work of*
> *man may justly aspire to such a title. It*
> *may nevertheless, perish in an hour by*
> *the folly, or corruption, or negligence of*
> *its only keepers, THE PEOPLE.*

To properly understand our history, we need to know as much as possible about the men who were involved in making that history. It was faith in the God of the Judeo-Christian Bible that drove America's earliest settlers to seek a place where they would have the freedom to live their lives and raise their children according to their deep-seated beliefs. Most of the Founding Fathers shared that same faith.

"The Founding Fathers were students of the Bible," pointed out John Eidsmoe in his well-researched book *Christianity and the Constitution.* According to Eidsmoe's research, fifty-two of the fifty-five delegates to the Constitutional Convention of 1787 were members of various Christian denominations. There was also "one lapsed Quaker and sometimes Anglican, and one [alleged] open Deist—Dr. Franklin, who attended every kind of Christian worship, called for public prayer, and contributed to all denominations."

"America is often called 'a Christian nation'

not because it was founded as such, but because its Founding Fathers were either Christians or had been influenced throughout their entire lives by the Christian consensus that surrounded them," Tim LaHaye said in his informative book *Faith of Our Founding Fathers*. "Christianity is a way of life. And that way of life had so permeated this nation by 1787 that it extended its influence to every area, including the fields of law, government, morality, marriage, and business."

Because of space limitations, I focused on the lives and words of twelve of the most prominent of the more than 200 men who came to be known as Founding Fathers. In order to provide an accurate description of their character and intent, I felt it was fundamentally important to include direct quotations from the men themselves that unambiguously illustrate their thinking about God, the Bible, the proper role of government, and the nature of man.

All Americans should find inspiration in the wisdom, character, and faith of the people who designed a government that has provided more freedom, more opportunities to excel, and a higher quality of life for its citizens than any other nation in recorded history.

Making certain young Americans understand their history and their godly heritage is vital to the future of the United States and to the memory of the God-fearing, Bible-believing men and women who created that heritage. As author Michael Crichton points out, "If you don't know history, you don't know anything. You're a leaf that doesn't know it's part of a tree."

Chapter One

Patrick Henry

Spirit of the Independence Movement

It cannot be emphasized too strongly or too often that this great nation was founded, not by religionists, but by Christians; not on religions, but on the Gospel of Jesus Christ. For this very reason people of other faiths have been afforded asylum, prosperity, and freedom of worship here.
PATRICK HENRY

On March 23, 1775, just twenty-seven days before "the shot heard 'round the world" was fired, Patrick Henry delivered a speech that ended with words that have become synonymous with his name: "Give me liberty or give me death!"

Much had been written and said in favor of American independence prior to Henry's famous exhortation. But historians have generally recognized that his passionate oration, in which he forcefully made the point that the colonies must now choose between freedom and slavery, was one of the most important events causing the smoldering embers of discontent to become a bonfire of revolution.

On April 19, the ongoing exchange of hot words and diplomatic wrangling between the thirteen colonies and the mother country was succeeded by an exchange of bullets and bombs during the battles of Lexington and Concord. That fateful day was immortalized by Ralph Waldo Emerson in his poem "Concord Hymn," in which he mentioned the "spirit that made those heroes dare to die, and leave their children free."

That spirit existed in abundance among the men we recognize as Founding Fathers, but two of them, Patrick Henry and Samuel Adams, have been honored with the special label "spirit of the independence movement." Both men were outspoken Christians who reflected the principle recorded in 2 Corinthians 3:17: "Where the Spirit of the Lord is, there is liberty."

Henry and Adams made frequent references to their belief that independence was God-ordained and that He would give them victory over a much stronger opponent, a conviction not universally shared by their fellow colonists. Although a substantial portion of the population had grave misgivings regarding armed rebellion against the British Empire, momentum in favor of separation reached critical mass following Henry's passionate exhortation, which he delivered following a couple of more conciliatory speeches by fellow delegates to the Virginia Convention. Every American should be familiar with Henry's brief but powerful words as recorded on March 23, 1775:

> *Mr. President: No man thinks more highly than I do of the patriotism, as well as abilities, of the very worthy gentlemen who have just addressed the House. But different men often see the same subject in different lights; and, therefore, I hope that it will not be thought disrespectful to those gentlemen, if entertaining as I do, opinions of a character very opposite to theirs, I shall speak forth my sentiments freely and without reserve. This is no time for ceremony. The question before the House is one of awful moment to this country. For my own part I consider it as nothing less than a question of freedom or slavery; and in proportion to the magnitude of the subject ought to be the freedom of the debate. It is only in this way that we can hope to arrive at truth, and fulfill the great responsibility which*

we hold to God and our country. Should I keep back my opinions at such a time, through fear of giving offense, I should consider myself guilty of treason toward my country, and of an act of disloyalty toward the majesty of heaven, which I revere above all earthly kings.

Mr. President, it is natural to man to indulge in the illusions of hope. We are apt to shut our eyes against a painful truth, and listen to the song of that siren, till she transforms us into beasts. Is this the part of wise men, engaged in great and arduous struggle for liberty? Are we disposed to be on the number of those who, having eyes, see not, and having ears, hear not, the things which so nearly concern their temporal salvation? For my part, whatever anguish of spirit it may cost, I am willing to know the whole truth; to know the worst and provide for it.

I have but one lamp by which my feet are guided; and that is the lamp of experience. I know of no way of judging of the future but by the past. And judging by the past I wish to know what there has been in the conduct of the British ministry for the last ten years to justify those hopes with which gentlemen have

*been pleased to solace themselves and
the House? Is it that insidious smile
with which our petition has been lately
received? Trust it not, sir; it will prove a
snare to your feet. Suffer not yourselves
to be betrayed with a kiss. Ask yourselves
how this gracious reception of our
petition comports with these warlike
preparations which cover our waters
and darken our land. Are fleets and
armies necessary to a work of love and
reconciliation? Have we shown ourselves
so unwilling to be reconciled, that force
must be called in to win back our love?
Let us not deceive ourselves, sir. These are
the implements of war and subjugation;
the last arguments to which kings resort.
I ask gentlemen, sir, what means this
martial array, if its purpose be not to
force us to submission? Can gentlemen
assign any other possible motives for it?
Has Great Britain any enemy, in this
quarter of the world, to call for all this
accumulation of navies and armies? No,
sir, she has none. They are meant for us;
they can be meant for no other.*

*They are sent over to bind and rivet
upon us those chains which the British
ministry have been so long forging. And*

*what have we to oppose them? Shall we
try argument? Sir, we have been trying
that for the last ten years. Have we
anything new to offer on the subject?*

*Nothing. We have held the subject up
in every light of which it is capable; but
it has been all in vain. Shall we resort
to entreaty and humble supplication?
What terms shall we find which have
not been already exhausted? Let us not, I
beseech you, sir, deceive ourselves longer.
Sir, we have done everything that could
be done to avert the storm which is now
coming on. We have petitioned; we have
remonstrated; we have supplicated;
we have prostrated ourselves before
the throne, and have implored its
interposition to arrest the tyrannical
hands of the ministry and parliament.
Our petitions have been slighted; our
remonstrances have produced additional
violence and insult; our supplications
have been disregarded; and we have
been spurned, with contempt, from the
foot of the throne. In vain, after these
things, may we indulge the fond hope
of peace and reconciliation. There is no
longer any room for hope. If we wish to
be free—if we mean to preserve inviolate*

*those inestimable privileges for which
we have been so long contending—if we
mean not basely to abandon the noble
struggle in which we have been so long
engaged, and which we have pledged
ourselves never to abandon until the
glorious object of our contest shall be
obtained, we must fight! I repeat it, sir,
we must fight! An appeal to arms and to
the God of Hosts is all that is left us!*

*They tell us, sir, that we are weak;
unable to cope with so formidable an
adversary. But when shall we be stronger?
Will it be the next week, or the next year?
Will it be when we are totally disarmed,
and when a British guard shall be
stationed in every house? Shall we gather
strength by irresolution and inaction?
Shall we acquire the means of effectual
resistance by lying supinely on our backs,
and hugging the delusive phantom of hope,
until our enemies shall have bound us
hand and foot? Sir, we are not weak, if we
make a proper use of the means which the
God of nature hath placed in our power.
Three millions of people, armed in the Holy
cause of Liberty, and in such a country as
that which we possess, are invincible by any
force which our enemy can send against us.*

Besides, sir, we shall not fight our battles alone. There is a just God who presides over the destinies of nations; and who will raise up friends to fight our battles for us. The battle, sir, is not to the strong alone; it is to the vigilant, the active, the brave. Besides, sir, we have no election. If we were base enough to desire it, it is now too late to retire from the contest. There is no retreat but in submission and slavery! Our chains are forged! Their clanking may be heard on the plains of Boston! The war is inevitable—and let it come! I repeat it, sir, let it come!

It is in vain, sir, to extenuate the matter. Gentlemen may cry peace, peace—but there is no peace. The war is actually begun! The next gale that sweeps from the North will bring to our ears the clash of resounding arms! Our brethren are already in the field! Why stand we here idle? What is it that gentlemen wish? What would they have? Is life so dear, or peace so sweet, as to be purchased at the price of chains and slavery? Forbid it, Almighty God! I know not what course others may take; but as for me, give me liberty or give me death!

Most in attendance were moved, and many shouted "To arms! To arms!" That included Thomas Jefferson, who later commented on Henry's speech in his autobiography: "I attended the debate at the door of the lobby of the House of Burgesses, and heard the splendid display of Mr. Henry's talents as a popular orator. They were great indeed; such as I have never heard from any other man. He appeared to speak as Homer wrote."

Henry's words leave no room for doubt regarding his belief in a vital link connecting biblical principles with proper governance. "It is when a people forget God that tyrants forge their chains," he said. "A vitiated state of morals, a corrupted public conscience, is incompatible with freedom. No free government, or the blessings of liberty, can be preserved to any people but by a firm adherence to justice, moderation, temperance, frugality, and virtue; and by a frequent recurrence to fundamental principles."

The fundamental principles to which Henry referred are those whose basis is found in the Judeo-Christian Bible. "The Bible," he said, "is a book worth more than all the other books that were ever printed."

"Virtue, morality, and religion. This is the armor, my friend, and this alone that renders us invincible. These are the tactics we should study. If we lose these, we are conquered, fallen indeed. . .so long as our manners and principles remain sound, there is no danger," Henry said.

Many who question the Christian faith of the Founding Fathers point to the issue of slavery as proof that they couldn't have been Christians— or at least not very good ones, since slavery was not outlawed in the Constitution. But many of the Founders, including Henry, George Washington, and Benjamin Franklin, did make reference to the shamefulness of the practice of forced slavery, but, regrettably, they understood there was a more urgent national priority—to produce a constitution that could be ratified. Because of the entrenched position of slave owners in a number of southern states, they understood that the chances of getting the required number of states to ratify a constitution that included the outlawing of slavery were nonexistent. For that reason, they made the pragmatic decision to sidestep that divisive issue until the overriding need of establishing a unified nation under an acceptable national constitution was achieved.

Speaking for himself, but representing the feelings of most of the Founders on the issue of slavery, Henry wrote:

> *Is it not amazing that at a time when the rights of humanity are defined and understood with precision, in a country, above all*

others, fond of liberty, that in such an age and in such a country we find men professing a religion the most humane, mild, gentle and generous, adopting a principle as repugnant to humanity as it is inconsistent with the Bible, and destructive to liberty? Every thinking, honest man rejects it in speculation; how few in practice from conscientious motives! . . . I believe a time will come when an opportunity will be offered to abolish this lamentable evil. Everything we do is to improve it, if it happens in our day; if not, let us transmit to our descendants, together with our slaves, a pity for their unhappy lot and an abhorrence of slavery. If we cannot reduce this wished-for reformation to practice, let us treat the unhappy victims with lenity. It is the furthest advance we can make toward justice. It is a debt we owe to the purity of our religion, to show that it is at variance with that law which warrants slavery.

Henry was born May 29, 1736, on a tobacco plantation in Studley, Hanover County, Virginia. Henry received much of his education from his aristocratic father, Colonel John Henry, and his mother, Sarah, whose ancestry included King Alfred the Great of Scotland and William the Conqueror.

Both of young Patrick's parents were descended from families that boasted a number of prominent orators, preachers, and statesmen. Henry credited the writings of a cousin, Dr. William Robertson, with influencing his attitudes regarding honesty, loyalty, and courage—all moral qualities he practiced and preached during his adult life.

Henry's formal education ended when he was removed from common school, as the colonial free public schools were called, at the age of ten. Under his father's tutelage, he was introduced to classic literature, the Bible, and the Greek and Latin languages. In addition to his interest in learning, Henry loved the outdoors and spent much of his youth hunting, fishing, and hiking.

Soon after Henry received his license to practice law in 1760, his name became well known, especially for his success in handling criminal cases. His reputation as a defender of colonial rights was enhanced by his involvement in a case in which he prevailed against King George III, which gave him a legal victory that helped him to become prominent in political circles.

Henry was elected as a delegate to the First Continental Congress in 1774 and to the Second Continental Congress in 1775. In 1776, he was elected to the first of his three terms as governor of Virginia.

Although elected as a delegate to the 1787 Constitutional Convention, Henry refused to attend because he believed a strong federal government would diminish many fundamental rights of the states. Once the Bill of Rights was added to the Constitution, however, he became reconciled to the advantages of a stronger federal government.

Along with so many of his fellow Founders, Patrick Henry was labeled a deist by some who apparently didn't know much about him. Here's his response to that charge: "Amongst other strange things said of me, I hear it is said by the deists that I am one of their number; and, indeed, that some good people think I am no Christian. This thought gives me much more pain than the appellation of Tory; because I think religion of infinitely higher importance than politics; and I find much cause to reproach myself that I have lived so long and have given no decided and public proofs of my being a Christian. But, indeed, this is a character which I prize far above all this world has, or can boast."

Further attesting to his deep religious beliefs, he wrote in his last will and testament, "This is all the inheritance I can give to my dear family. The religion of Christ can give them one which will make them rich indeed."

Chapter Two

Samuel Adams

Father of the American Revolution

*I could say a thousand things to you, if I had
leisure. I could dwell on the importance of
piety and religion, of industry and frugality,
of prudence, economy, regularity and even
Government, all of which are essential to the
well being of a family. But I have not time.
I cannot however help repeating piety,
because I think it indispensable. Religion
in a family is at once its brightest
ornament and its best security.*
SAMUEL ADAMS

Samuel Adams was one of the earliest and most
effective of the Founding Fathers in building support for colonial independence and in generating
opposition to the English Parliament's every

provocation. Those activities earned Adams the title "Father of the American Revolution."

In terms of population, the prospect of war against the British looked like a David versus Goliath situation, and there was much to support that characterization. By 1770, the population of the Colonies was approximately 2.5 million, 20 percent of whom were slaves, while the combined population of the British Isles totaled approximately 9 million. Adams didn't see that as an insurmountable problem. "It does not take a majority to prevail," he said, "but rather an irate, tireless minority, keen on setting brushfires of freedom in the minds of men." Adams himself was an irate and tireless setter of brushfires that eventually brought freedom to his beloved country.

British leaders understood the dynamic role Adams played in the independence movement so well that General Thomas Gage, in an effort to end hostilities with the colonists before they began, offered pardons to all rebels except for Adams and John Hancock "whose offenses are of too flagitious nature to admit of any other consideration than that of condign punishment."

General Gage also tried bribery as a method of silencing Adams, offering him "great gifts and advancement" if he would stop agitating the Colonists. Adams indignantly refused. That incident was recorded in historian B.J. Lossing's *The Signers of the Declaration of Independence:*

> *When the governor was asked why Mr.*
> *Adams had not been silenced by office, he*
> *replied, that "such obstinacy and inflexible*
> *disposition of the man, that he can never be*
> *conciliated by any office or gift whatever."*
> *And when, in 1774, Governor Gage,*
> *by authority of ministers, sent Colonel*
> *Fenton to offer Adams a magnificent*
> *consideration if he would cease his hostility*
> *to government, or menace him with*
> *all the evils of attainder, that inflexible*
> *patriot gave this remarkable answer to*
> *Fenton: "I trust I have long since made my*
> *peace with the King of kings. No personal*
> *consideration shall induce me to abandon*
> *the righteous cause of my country. Tell*
> *Governor Gage, it is the advice of Samuel*
> *Adams to him, no longer to insult the*
> *feelings of an exasperated people."*

Adams first began to attract the attention of King George and Parliament in 1764, when he took a strong public stand against enforcement of the Sugar and Molasses Acts, which imposed shipment restrictions and high taxes on those commodities imported into the English colonies. Those unprecedented taxes were the first economic acts by the

British that incited serious consideration of independence among the colonists.

Adding fuel to the fire, in 1765 the British Parliament passed the Stamp Act, which imposed a tax on all legal documents, newspapers, pamphlets, and even playing cards. The tax was denounced as "taxation without representation," an effective rallying cry that influenced many to join the movement for independence. Formed to oppose the Stamp Act, the Sons of Liberty, a rapidly growing patriotic society, made it difficult, if not impossible, through a campaign of physical violence, to distribute the stamps. Adams and Paul Revere headed the Boston chapter.

Adams was also the motivating force behind formation of the Stamp Act Congress, which convened in New York specifically to develop a plan of resistance to the infuriating tax. The Sons of Liberty successfully organized colonial merchants in opposing the importation of British merchandise, a boycott that resulted in a substantial reduction in the volume of British goods coming into the colonies. Although Parliament repealed the Stamp Act in 1766, it is still seen today as one of the major causes of the American Revolution.

With encouragement from the Sons of Liberty, Committees of Correspondence began to appear throughout the colonies. Originally, such Committees had been established as a way for colonial legislatures to communicate with each other, but now they became essential tools for shaping public opinion and for generating opposition to British rule. They were also successful in generating an important sense of interdependence and identity throughout the colonies. For the first time, the revolutionary-minded colonists were able to develop a unified policy of resistance.

Adams's extensive writings contributed to his reputation as a persistent promoter of the call to revolution. "If ye love wealth better than liberty," Adams wrote, "the tranquility of servitude than the animating contest of freedom, go from us in peace. We ask not your counsels or arms. Crouch down and lick the hands which feed you. May your chains sit lightly upon you, and may posterity forget that ye were our countrymen!"

Most of his writings appeared originally in the *Boston Gazette*, a large circulation newspaper for its time. In 1772, the *Gazette* published Adams's "The Rights of the Colonists," in which he emphasized this tenet of the revolution: "The right to freedom being the gift of the Almighty. . . . The rights of Colonists as Christians. . .may be best understood by reading and carefully studying the institution of The Great Law Giver and Head of the Christian Church, which are to be found clearly written and promulgated in the New Testament."

To dramatize abhorrence generated by the Tea Act the British Parliament passed on May 10, 1763, Adams instigated an event the world knows today as the Boston Tea Party. On December 16, 1773, colonists dressed as Native Americans dumped three shiploads of English tea into Boston Harbor.

Passage by the British Parliament in 1774 of four laws designed as punishment for the Boston Tea Party, known to the colonists as the Intolerable Acts, provided the impetus for convening a Colonial Congress. The four punitive acts were the Boston Port Act, which closed Boston to trade; the Massachusetts Government Act, which revoked the Colony's charter; the Quartering Act, which required Colonists to provide quartering for British soldiers; and the Impartial Administration of Justice Act, which removed British officials from the jurisdiction of Massachusetts courts.

In recognition of his leadership role in generating support for establishment of a general congress, Adams was elected as a delegate to the First Continental Congress, which convened on September 5, 1774. Delegates to the First Continental Congress called for a second congress to be convened on May 10, 1775, if the British persisted in their "Coercive Acts," another popular name for the 1774 Parliamentary measures the colonists considered intolerable. Prior to that date, the die had already been cast by a number of events, including the intransigence of Parliament and the battles of Lexington and Concord.

Facing the growing crisis, the Second Continental Congress was convened as scheduled, with Adams again serving as a delegate. The primary responsibilities of the congress were threefold: to formulate and oversee the conduct of the war, to advance and preserve the newly formed "union" of the thirteen colonies, and to develop a governing document to guide the emerging independent country. Virginia delegate George Washington was commissioned to organize and command a Continental Army. Committees were established to generate plans for the conduct of international trade, to develop fiscal policies, and to find ways to seek much-needed military and financial assistance from overseas.

Developing a rudimentary constitution proved to be tedious and contentious work, with Congress finally reaching agreement on the Articles of Confederation on November 15, 1777. It then took more than three years from the time the congressional delegates approved the Articles before the colonies officially ratified them. In the meantime, the Second Continental Congress approved the Declaration of Independence on July 2, 1776, and formally adopted it two days later—though all the signatures weren't collected until August 2.

At the signing of the Declaration, Adams said,

"We have this day restored the Sovereign to Whom all men ought to be obedient. He reigns in heaven and from the rising to the setting of the sun, let His kingdom come." Also in reference to the Declaration, Adams said, "The people seem to recognize this as though it were a decree promulgated from heaven."

Adams spoke often regarding the importance of character and public morality: "A general dissolution of principles and manners will more surely overthrow the liberties of America than the whole force of the common enemy," he said. "While the people are virtuous they cannot be subdued; but when once they lose their virtue they will be ready to surrender their liberties to the first external or internal invader. If virtue and knowledge are diffused among the people, they will never be enslaved. This will be their great security."

Adams believed strongly in educating young people about God and morality: "Let divines and philosophers, statesmen and patriots, unite their endeavors to renovate the age, by impressing the minds of men with the importance of educating their little boys and girls, of inculcating in the minds of youth the fear and love of the Deity and universal philanthropy, and, in subordination to these great principles, the love of their country; of instructing them in the art of self-government without which they never can act a wise part in the government of societies, great or small; in short, of leading them in the study and practice of the exalted virtues of the Christian system."

Lossing described Adams's ubiquitous role as a driving force for American independence in his authoritative 1848 book:

> *The journals of Congress during that time show his name upon almost every important committee of that body. And probably no man did more toward bringing about the American Revolution, and in effecting the independence of the Colonies, than Samuel Adams. He was the first to assert boldly those political truths upon which rested the whole superstructure of our confederacy—he was the first to act in support of those truths—and when, in the General Council of States, independence was proposed, and the timid faltered, and the over-prudent hesitated, the voice of Samuel Adams was ever loudest in denunciations of a temporizing policy, and also in the utterance of strong encouragement to the fainthearted. "I should advise," he said on one occasion, "persisting in our struggle for liberty,*

> though it were revealed from Heaven
> that nine hundred and ninety-nine were
> to perish, and only one of a thousand
> were to survive and retain his liberty!
> One such freeman must possess more
> virtue, and enjoy more happiness, than
> a thousand slaves; and let him propagate
> his like, and transmit to them what he
> hath so nobly preserved."

One of Samuel Adams's strongest statements of his faith was included in his will: "Principally, and first of all, I resign my soul to the Almighty Being who gave it, and my body I commit to the dust, relying on the merits of Jesus Christ for the pardon of my sins."

Adams was known to some of his contemporaries as "the last Puritan," a term that has become a pejorative in the minds of many today. To Adams, though, it was high praise.

Chapter Three

John Adams
Atlas of American Independence

*Suppose a nation in some distant region
should take the Bible for their only law book
and every member should regulate his conduct
by the precepts there exhibited! Every member
would be obliged in conscience to temperance,
frugality, and industry; to justice, kindness,
and charity towards his fellow men; and to
piety, love, and reverence toward Almighty
God. What a Eutopia, what a Paradise
would this region be.*
JOHN ADAMS

Richard Stockton, a friend and fellow signer of the
Declaration of Independence, labeled John Adams
"The Atlas of American Independence" because
of the heavy burden Adams shouldered as one of

the most notable leaders in shaping and advancing policies and events that led to freedom for their beloved homeland.

Regarding Adams's intellect and the role he played in the independence movement, Clemson University professor Bradley Thompson wrote:

> *Adams witnessed the American Revolution from beginning to end. In 1761 he assisted James Otis in defending Boston merchants against enforcement of Britain's Sugar Act. Gradually, Adams became a key leader of the radical political movement in Boston and one of the earliest and most principled voices for independence at the Continental Congress. Likewise, as a public intellectual, he wrote some of the most important and influential essays, constitutions, and treatises of the Revolutionary period movement. John Adams exemplifies the mind of the American Revolution.*

Adams had been in favor of early attempts at reconciliation with England, but that changed irrevocably following the Boston Tea Party in 1773. From that point on, Adams was staunchly committed to the cause of American independence. By 1774, Adams urged his fellow Americans to adopt "revolution principles"—a resolve to do what had to be done in order to guarantee American rights and liberties.

Because the power of his intellect and the quality of his writing had become well known among his fellow rebels, Adams was one of five men chosen to draft the Declaration of Independence—along with Thomas Jeff son, Benjamin Franklin, Roger Sherman, and Robert R. Livingston. It was Adams who insisted that Jefferson produce the original draft, after the committee members narrowed it down to the two of them. When Jefferson completed the Declaration, Adams became its most articulate and passionate presenter as the document was unveiled to the assembled members of the Second Continental Congress. Following a speech Adams delivered on the floor of Congress in support of independence, Jefferson used the word *colossus* to describe him.

In that speech, Adams spoke as a prophet:

> *The second day of July, 1776, will be the most memorable epoch in the history of America, to be celebrated by succeeding generations as the great anniversary festival, commemorated as the day of deliverance by solemn acts of devotion to God Almighty from one end of the Continent to the other, from this time*

*forward forevermore. You will think
me transported with enthusiasm, but I
am not. I am well aware of the toil, the
blood, and treasure that it will cost us to
maintain this Declaration and support
and defend these states; yet, through all
the gloom, I can see the rays of light and
glory; that the end is worth all the means;
that posterity will triumph in that day's
transaction, even though we shall rue it,
which I trust in God we shall not.*

The Declaration of Independence was proclaimed on July 2 but wasn't officially signed until July 4, a day Adams said later "will be celebrated by succeeding generations as the day of deliverance with pomp and parade, with guns, bells, bonfires, and illuminations, from one end of this continent to the other."

Adams was born October 19, 1735, in Braintree (now Quincy), Massachusetts, where he received his primary and secondary schooling. Entering Harvard at the age of sixteen, he graduated in 1755 then became a teacher while he continued studying law. Adams began his law practice in Braintree before moving on to Boston where he made the acquaintance of many influential men with whom he would later be actively engaged in the quest for independence. It was there that he established himself as one of the colonies' most respected lawyers and constitutional scholars.

In 1764, Adams married Abigail Smith, a pastor's daughter. During their fifty-four-year marriage, Abigail was a strong source of support for her husband's role in the rebellion as evinced by many of her writings, many of which have become important historical documents. Between 1774 and 1784, they exchanged hundreds of letters that shed much light on their close relationship and the extraordinary times during which they lived.

In a letter written to Abigail dated September 16, 1774, Adams recounted this experience:

> *When the Congress first met, Mr.*
> *Cushing made a motion that it should*
> *be opened with prayer. It was opposed by*
> *Mr. Jay, of New York, and Mr. Rutledge*
> *of South Carolina, because we were so*
> *divided in religious sentiments, some*
> *Episcopalians, some Quakers, some*
> *Anabaptists, some Presbyterians, and*
> *some Congregationalists, that we could*
> *not join the same act of worship. Mr.*
> *Samuel Adams arose and said he was*
> *no bigot, and could hear a prayer from a*
> *gentleman of piety and virtue, who was*
> *at the same time a friend to his country.*

*He was a stranger in Philadelphia, but
had heard that Mr. Duche (Dushay they
pronounce it) deserved that character, and
therefore he moved that Mr. Duche, an
Episcopal clergyman, might be desired to
read prayers to the Congress, tomorrow
morning. The motion was seconded and
passed in the affirmative. Mr. Randolph,
our president waited on Mr. Duche,
and received for an answer that if his
health would permit he certainly would.
Accordingly, next morning he appeared
with his clerk and in his pontificals, and
read several prayers in the established
form; and then read the Collect for the
seventh day of September, which was the
thirty-fifth Psalm. You must remember
this was the next morning after we heard
the horrible rumor of the cannonade of
Boston. I never saw a greater effect upon
an audience. It seemed as if Heaven had
ordained that Psalm to be read on that
morning.*

*After this Mr. Duche, unexpected to
everybody, struck out into an extemporary
prayer, which filled the bosom of every
man present. I must confess I never heard
a better prayer, or one so well pronounced.
Episcopalian as he is, Dr. Cooper himself*

(Dr. Samuel Cooper, well known as a zealous patriot and pastor of the church in Brattle Square, Boston) never prayed with such fervor, such earnestness and pathos, and in language so elegant and sublime— for America, for Congress, for the Province of Massachusetts Bay, and especially the town of Boston. It has had an excellent effect upon everybody here. I must beg you to read that Psalm. If there was any faith in the Sortes Biblicae, it would be thought providential.

It will amuse your friends to read this letter and the thirty-fifth Psalm to them. Read it to your father and Mr. Wibird. I wonder what our Braintree Churchmen will think of this! Mr. Duche is one of the most ingenious men, and best characters, and greatest orators in the Episcopal order, upon this continent. Yet a zealous friend of Liberty and his country.

Psalm 35, which was often used as a prayer during the critical period of time leading up to the Revolutionary War, was timely, indeed, especially verses 1–10 (NASB):

Contend, O Lord, with those who contend with me;
Fight against those who fight against me.

Take hold of buckler and shield,
And rise up for my help.
Draw also the spear and the battle-axe to meet
those who pursue me;
Say to my soul, "I am your salvation."
Let those be ashamed and dishonored who seek
my life;
Let those be turned back and humiliated who
devise evil against me.
Let them be like chaff before the wind,
With the angel of the Lord driving them on.
Let their way be dark and slippery,
With the angel of the Lord pursuing them.
For without cause they hid their net for me;
Without cause they dug a pit for my soul.
Let destruction come upon him, unawares;
And let the net which he hid catch himself;
Into that very destruction let him fall.
And my soul shall rejoice in the Lord;
It shall exult in His salvation.
All my bones will say,
"Lord, who is like Thee,
Who delivers the afflicted from him who is too
strong for him,
And the afflicted and the needy from him who
robs him?"

Abigail Adams's own writings reflect her strong belief in the God of the Bible, to whom she often referred as she did in this letter to her husband: "I feel no anxiety at the large armament designed against us. The remarkable interpositions of heaven in our favor cannot be too gratefully acknowledged. He who fed the Israelites in the wilderness, who clothes the lilies of the field and who feeds the young ravens when they cry, will not forsake a people engaged in so right a cause, if we remember His loving kindness."

John and Abigail were members of the Congregational Church at Brattle Square in Boston. When in Philadelphia, Adams, along with his friend and fellow Founder Benjamin Rush, regularly attended worship services at the Old Pine Presbyterian Church where they enjoyed the sermons of Reverend George Duffield, who openly supported the American Revolution. (In 1776, Duffield was named Chaplain to the Continental Congress.)

When the Second Continental Congress convened on May 10, 1775, Adams was selected chairman of the Board of War and Ordnance, the committee primarily responsible for conducting the Revolutionary War. When Congress authorized the establishment of a Continental Army, Adams nominated George Washington to be its commanding general, a move that turned out to be one of the most important decisions of the independence movement.

In 1779, after serving nearly two years on a diplomatic mission to France, Adams returned to his home in Massachusetts, where he played a leading role in the convention that produced the Massachusetts Constitution. That document became a model for a number of other state constitutions and, a few years later, was influential in shaping the Federal Constitution.

Adams was elected to the first of his two terms as vice president of the United States in 1789, finishing second to George Washington in total number of electoral votes cast for president. According to the system in place at that time, the candidate receiving the most votes became president and the person receiving the next highest number of votes became vice president.

As originally conceived, the office of vice president was intended primarily as a means of providing a successor in the event of the president's death or incapacitation. The industrious Adams called the vice presidency "the most insignificant office that ever the invention of man contrived."

When President Washington decided not to run for a third term in 1796, Adams, Jefferson, Aaron Burr, and Thomas Pinckney each declared his candidacy. Adams and Pinckney were Federalists while Jefferson and Burr were Republicans, a party that later came to be known as the Democratic-Republican Party. They were also known as anti-Federalists because of their opposition to what they considered to be too much centralization of power in a national government. The election of 1796 was, for all practical purposes, the beginning of our two-party political system, an approach Washington opposed because he didn't like the idea of dividing the country into partisan groups.

As winner of the largest number of electoral votes, Adams became the second president of the United States, and Jefferson, recipient of the second largest number, became vice president. This was the only time in U.S. history when a president and vice president from opposing political parties occupied the top two elected offices.

Adams was inaugurated on March 4, 1797, in Philadelphia, before the nation's capital was moved to Washington, D.C. He moved into the unfinished White House on November 1, 1800. The day after he took up his new residency, Adams wrote a letter to Abigail in which he included the following prayer: "I Pray Heaven to bestow THE BEST OF BLESSINGS ON This House and All that shall hereafter Inhabit it, May no one but Honest and Wise Men ever rule under This Roof." His prayer can still be seen engraved upon the mantel of the White House State Dining Room.

After Adams lost the 1800 election to Jefferson, the two Founding Fathers became bitter rivals until their reconciliation in 1812, when they began a correspondence that has been characterized as "the most impressive in the history of American letters." In a letter to Jefferson after the death of Abigail, Adams said, "That you and I shall meet in a better world I have no doubt than we now exist on the same globe; if my reason did not convince me of this, Cicero's Dream of Scipio, and his Essay on Friendship and Old Age would have been sufficient for that purpose. But Jesus taught us that a future state is a social state, when He promised to prepare places in His Father's house of many mansions, for His disciples."

Both men died on July 4, 1826, within hours of each other.

Evidence of Adams's strong belief in the importance of the Christian religion and biblical principles as the foundation upon which the United States of America rests appears over and over again in his writings. "The general principles on which the fathers achieved independence were the general principles of Christianity," Adams wrote in a letter to Jefferson. "I will avow that I then believed, and now believe, that those general principles of Christianity are as eternal and immutable as the existence and attributes of God; and that those principles of liberty are as unalterable as human nature."

John Adams practiced what he preached.

Chapter Four

George Washington
Father of Our Country

*It is impossible to account for the creation
of the universe, without the agency of a
Supreme Being. It is impossible to govern the
universe without the aid of a Supreme
Being. It is impossible to reason without
arriving at a Supreme Being.*
GEORGE WASHINGTON

Similarities between David, king of ancient Israel,
and George Washington are striking among people
familiar with the Judeo-Christian Bible and with
early U.S. history. David, under God's direction
and protection, led the forces that established Israel as a sovereign nation, and Washington, first
as a military leader and later as a statesman and

political leader, was instrumental in securing nationhood for the United States of America.

It doesn't take much imagination to liken the contest between colonial America and Great Britain to the battle between little David and gigantic Goliath. Eyewitness accounts of Washington's seemingly miraculous deliverance in battle have led many to believe he was the beneficiary of the same supernatural protection as King David.

Just as David was convinced he was being guided and protected by the invisible hand of God, so Washington believed God would intervene on his and America's behalf. No one who has read much about Washington can deny that he, like David, was devoted to his God and that he, again like David, spent much time in prayer. In that respect, Washington and the king of Israel can be seen as "men after God's own heart."

Washington was born into a Christian family on February 22, 1732, in Westmoreland County, Virginia. Washington's father was described as "a man of monumental proportions, a figure of great energy, and an established member of the Virginia gentry." Augustine Washington's prominence opened doors of opportunity for his sons.

While still a teenager, George Washington was appointed surveyor for Culpeper County. In that capacity, he worked in frontier areas of Virginia, an experience that taught him much about problems involved in the advancement of civilization into undeveloped areas of the country. That exposure, plus the military experience he acquired while serving in Virginia's militia, would serve him well in the future.

Later, as a colonel in the British Army, Washington was appointed as an aide to General Edward Braddock during the French and Indian War. He spent three years in that position, all the while learning about the principles and responsibilities of a professional army officer. Eventually, Washington was given authority over British forces responsible for defending Virginia's frontier.

An event that seemed to confirm Washington's special destiny occurred during the 1755 Battle of the Monongahela, when General Braddock's forces "were being annihilated," according to an account that was once included in American textbooks. During that fierce battle, Washington "rode back and forth among the troops delivering General Braddock's orders. As the battle raged, every officer on horseback, except Washington, was shot down. Even General Braddock was killed at which point the troops fled in confusion."

A few days later, Washington confirmed in a letter to his brother his belief that he had been supernaturally protected: "But by the all-powerful dispensations of Providence, I have been protected beyond all human probability or expectation; for I had four bullets through my coat, and two horses shot under me, yet escaped unhurt, although death was leveling my companions on every side of me."

After resigning from the militia in 1759, Washington gained insight into legislative procedures and practices by serving in the House of Burgesses, the first assembly of elected representatives of the English colonists in North America. As events unfolded from 1759 to 1774, Washington became convinced that independence from Great Britain would soon become necessary. He then joined the "revolutionary" legislature and became one of Virginia's delegates to the First Continental Congress and, a year later, to the Second Continental Congress.

When it was decided that a Continental Army should be formed by bringing various militia and regular regiments together, Washington was selected to be its commander. His first task was to organize and train the disparate groups from which he was charged with creating an effective army.

As a point of beginning, Washington placed great importance and emphasis upon godly behavior. He established what was to become the Chaplain Corps and made attendance at regular worship services mandatory. His first general order read: "The General most earnestly requires and expects a due observance of those articles of war established for the government of the army, which forbid profane cursing, swearing, and drunkenness. And in like manner he requires and expects of all officers and soldiers, not engaged in actual duty, a punctual attendance on Divine service, to implore the blessing of Heaven upon the means used for our safety and defense."

Washington's recorded words as the colonists prepared for war against the world's most powerful empire are laced with references to the necessity of dependence upon God. Prior to the beginning of hostilities, he exhorted his troops: "The time is now near at hand which must probably determine whether Americans are to be freemen or slaves; whether they are to have any property they can call their own; whether their houses and farms are to be pillaged and destroyed, and themselves consigned to a state of wretchedness from which no human efforts will deliver them. The fate of unborn millions will now depend, under God, on the courage of this army. Our cruel and unrelenting enemy leaves us only the choice of brave resistance, or the most abject submission. We have, therefore to resolve to conquer or die."

In 1778, when the fortunes of war began to turn in the colonists' favor, Washington told his troops, "The instances of Providential goodness which we have experienced and which have now almost crowned our labors with complete success demand from us in a peculiar manner the warmest returns of gratitude and piety to the Supreme Author of all good."

Later that year, in a letter to General Thomas Nelson, Washington wrote, "The hand of providence has been so conspicuous in all this [the course of the war] that he must be worse than an infidel that lacks faith, and more wicked that has not gratitude to acknowledge his obligations; but it will be time enough for me to turn Preacher when my present appointment ceases."

When the Treaty of Paris was signed in 1783, officially ending the Revolutionary War, Washington resigned his military commission and returned to private life as a farmer on his Mount Vernon estate. But he soon became concerned about inherent weakness in the Articles of Confederation as a document capable of meeting the needs of the new nation. Washington, along with many other influential leaders, began to understand the necessity of a stronger central government to further unite the thirteen sovereign states, each of which was governed separately.

Under the Articles of Confederation, there were no effective provisions for the establishment of a national defense, nor were there any mechanisms through which taxes could be assessed or collected from the states. As commander in chief during the Revolutionary War, Washington had become especially sensitive to monetary problems, since his troops were too often without adequate clothing, food, weapons, and medicine.

Soon after the Constitutional Convention opened on May 25, 1787, Washington was chosen by unanimous vote to become its president. Washington was well known and universally respected; it has been speculated that he was the only individual who could have held the convention, with all the emotionally charged issues that would be put forward by the geographically diverse delegations, together.

By September of 1787, the assembled delegates had, under Washington's quiet but firm leadership, produced a new U.S. Constitution. Seven months later, Washington, by action of the Electoral College, was inaugurated as America's first president.

Prior to his inauguration, a newspaper announcement regarding the event said, "On the morning of the day on which our illustrious President will be invested with his office, the bells will ring at nine o'clock, when the people may go up and in a solemn manner commit the new Government, with its important train of consequences, to the holy protection and blessings of the Most High. An early hour is prudently fixed for this peculiar act of devotion, and it is designed wholly for prayer."

Once again referencing his belief in God's hand in establishing the United States of America, Washington, in his inaugural address, said:

Such being the impressions under which I have, in obedience to the public summons, repaired to the present station, it would be peculiarly improper to omit, in this first official act, my fervent supplications to that Almighty Being who rules over the universe, who presides in the councils of nations and whose providential aids can supply every human defect. . . .

No people can be bound to acknowledge and adore the Invisible Hand which conducts the affairs of men more than the people of the United States. Every step by which they have advanced to the character of an independent nation seems to have been distinguished by some token of providential agency; And in the important revolution just accomplished in the system of their United government, the tranquil deliberations and voluntary consent of so many distinct communities, from which the event has resulted can not be compared with the means by which most governments have been established, without some return of pious gratitude, along with an humble anticipation of the future blessings which the past seems to presage.

These reflections, arising out of the present crisis, have forced themselves too strongly on my mind to be suppressed. You will join with me I trust in thinking that there are none under the influence of which the proceedings of a new and free Government can more auspiciously commence.

We ought to be no less persuaded that the propitious smiles of Heaven can never be expected on a nation that disregards the eternal rules of order and right which Heaven itself has ordained; and since the preservation of the sacred fire of liberty and the destiny of the republican model of government are justly considered as deeply, perhaps finally, staked of the experiment.

Washington essentially "invented" the office of president of the United States during his first term. Upon assuming the presidency, he said, "I walk on untrodden ground. There is scarcely any part of my conduct that may not hereafter be drawn into precedent."

When announcing his decision not to run for

a third term, Washington took advantage of one more opportunity to remind the nation of the importance of religion and morality and their link with national security, domestic tranquility, and the rights of individuals. In his Farewell Address, he said:

> *Of all the dispositions and habits which lead to political prosperity, Religion and Morality are indispensable supports. In vain would that man claim the tribute of Patriotism, who should labor to subvert these great pillars of human happiness, these firmest props of the duties of Men and Citizens. The mere Politician, equally with the pious man, ought to respect and cherish them. A volume could not trace all their connections with private and public felicity. Let it simply be asked, where is the security for property, for reputation, for life, if the sense of religious obligation desert the oaths which are the instrument of investigation in Courts of Justice? And let us with caution indulge the supposition that morality can be maintained without religion. Whatever may be conceded to the influence of refined education on minds of peculiar structure, reason and experience both*

*forbid us to expect that national moral-
ity can prevail in exclusion of religious
principle.*

*It is substantially true that virtue or
morality is a necessary spring of popular
government. The rule, indeed, extends
with more or less force to every species of
free government. Who, that is a sincere
friend to it, can look with indifference
upon attempts to shake the foundation of
the fabric?*

While some have maintained that Washington
was not a church member, biographical informa-
tion confirming his regular church attendance
abounds, including his Prayer for the United States
of America, which appears on a plaque in St. Paul's
Chapel in New York City, as well as at Pohick
Church in Fairfax County, where Washington was
a vestryman from 1762 to 1784:

*Almighty God; We make our earnest
prayer that Thou wilt keep the United
States in Thy Holy protection; and Thou
wilt incline the hearts of the Citizens
to cultivate a spirit of subordination
and obedience to Government; and
entertain a brotherly affection and love
for one another and for their fellow*

> Citizens of the United States at large, and
> particularly for their brethren who have
> served in the Field.
>
> And finally that Thou wilt most
> graciously be pleased to dispose us all to
> do justice, to love mercy, and to demean
> ourselves with that Charity, humility,
> and pacific temper of mind which were
> the Characteristics of the Divine Author
> of our blessed Religion, and without a
> humble imitation of whose example in
> these things we can never hope to be a
> happy nation. Grant our supplication, we
> beseech Thee, through Jesus Christ our
> Lord. Amen.

In his well-researched book *Faith of Our Founding Fathers*, best-selling author Tim LaHaye presents excerpts from Washington's personal prayer book with this lead-in: "That President George Washington was a devout believer in Jesus Christ and had accepted Him as his Lord and Savior is easily demonstrated by a reading of his personal prayer book (written in his own handwriting), which was discovered in 1891 among a collection of his papers. To date no historian has questioned its authenticity."

Jared Sparks, the nineteenth-century historian, authored a twelve-volume collection of Washington's writings. He summarized Washington's character and religious beliefs in this brief statement:

> *A Christian in faith and practice, he was habitually devout. His reverence for religion is seen in his example, his public communications, and his private writings. He uniformly ascribed his successes to the beneficent agency of the Supreme Being.*
>
> *Charitable and humane, he was liberal to the poor and kind to those in distress. As a husband, son, and brother, he was tender and affectionate.*
>
> *If a man spoke, wrote, and acted as a Christian through a long life, who gave numerous proofs of his believing himself to be such, and who was never known to say, write or do a thing contrary to his professions, if such a man is not to be ranked among the believers of Christianity, it would be impossible to establish the point by any grain of reasoning.*

Looking at all the evidence, it is difficult, if not impossible, to believe Washington was anything but a Bible-believing Christian.

Chapter Five

Thomas Jefferson
Author of the Declaration of Independence

> *My views are the result of a life of inquiry*
> *and reflection, and very different from the*
> *anti-Christian system imputed to me by*
> *those who know nothing of my opinions. To*
> *the corruptions of Christianity I am, indeed*
> *opposed; but not to the genuine precepts*
> *of Jesus himself. I am a Christian in the*
> *only sense in which he wished any one to*
> *be; sincerely attached to his doctrines in*
> *preference to all others.*
> THOMAS JEFFERSON

Of all the great men who built this nation, Thomas Jefferson might be the one least expected to appear in a book on the Founders' Christian beliefs.

But in my opinion, Jefferson's own words help

to refute the claims of many today who hold that he was a deist or agnostic rather than a Bible-believing Christian. It makes much more sense to base an understanding of Jefferson's religious and political beliefs on what he said about himself rather than on assertions made by those with agendas other than to tell the truth about him.

No one disputes the fact that Jefferson was intrigued by the Bible and that he studied it carefully. Because of the time he devoted to that study, he undoubtedly understood the "precepts of Jesus," among which are Jesus' statements regarding His own divinity, a basic idea by which Christians are identified.

"No great American, not even Lincoln," says historian Clyde N. Wilson, "has been put to so many contradictory uses by later generations of enemies and apologists, and therefore none has undergone so much distortion. In fact, most of what has been asserted about Jefferson in the last hundred years—and even more of what has been implied or assumed about him—is so lacking in context and proportion as to be essentially false. What we commonly see is not Jefferson. It is a strange amalgam or composite in which the misconceptions of each succeeding generation have been combined until the original is no longer discernible."

There is some controversy about the extent to

which Jefferson believed in the inerrancy of the Bible, but the issue may never be resolved—his writings over a long life show some inconsistencies on the subject. As to his views on Jesus, the editor of *The Real Thomas Jefferson,* a book that contains 330 pages of quotations by the third president, notes that "toward the end of his life, Jefferson apparently changed his mind about the divinity of Jesus. The letters he wrote during his final years contain occasional references to 'our Savior.'"

On several occasions, Jefferson mentioned "a God who presides above the destinies of nations." Deists believe no such thing. By definition, they deny the concept of a Creator actively involved in the lives of individuals and nations. Jefferson's own words offer proof that he believed God took an interest in His creation and that He influenced the outcome of history. Many biographers have mentioned the fact that Jefferson made it a daily practice to pray and read his Bible, activities not associated with deists and agnostics, who would find such activities a waste of time.

In the Declaration of Independence, Jefferson wrote: "When in the Course of human Events, it becomes necessary for one People to dissolve the Political Bonds which have connected them with another, and to assume among the Powers of the Earth, the separate and equal Station to which the *Laws of Nature and of Nature's God* entitle them. . . ."

Jefferson's fellow Founders understood that "Nature's God" and the Judeo-Christian God of the Bible, also referred to as *Lord*, were one and the same. Throughout his presidency, Jefferson signed all official documents "In the year of our Lord." It was Jefferson who recommended that the Great Seal of the United States depict a Bible story and include God in the national motto.

Jefferson approved money out of the Federal Treasury for the support of a Christian missionary program to the Native Americans and for the construction of a Christian church in which they could worship. As president and head of the Washington D.C. public school system, Jefferson mandated that a Bible and a hymnbook be placed in each classroom. He described the Bible as "the cornerstone of liberty. . . . I have always said, I will always say, that studious perusal of the sacred volume will make better citizens, better fathers, better husbands."

Jefferson's now-famous phrase "separation of church and state" appeared in a letter he sent to a Baptist congregation to assure them the First Amendment would *not* allow establishment of a state-controlled denomination, such as the mother country had in the Church of England. Along with the Founders involved in producing the First Amendment, he clearly intended for the government to be *completely* neutral where religious issues were concerned.

"Every religious society has a right to determine for itself the times for these exercises, and the objects proper for them, according to their own particular tenets," Jefferson said.

Despite assertions to the contrary, the phrase "separation of church and state" is not now and never was part of the U.S. Constitution, including the First Amendment. That phrase may have had its roots in a letter written years earlier by Roger Sherman, signer of the Declaration of Independence, The Articles of Confederation, and The U.S. Constitution. He wrote: "(W)hen they have opened a gap in the hedge or *wall of separation* between the garden of the church and the wilderness of the world, God hath ever broke down the wall itself, removed the candlestick, and made His garden a wilderness, as at this day. And that therefore if He will ever please to restore His garden and paradise again, it must of necessity be walled in peculiarly unto Himself from the world."

In other words, Sherman was saying the church must not allow the world to corrupt its holiness; its freedom must not be infringed upon by the state.

Throughout Jefferson's life, those who knew him best considered him to be a man of the highest moral character. Excerpts from a letter written by his grandson, Thomas Jefferson Randolph, to biographer Henry S. Randall, provide an eyewitness report on the personal life and character of Jefferson:

> *Dear Sir: In compliance with your request, I have committed to paper my reminiscences of Mr. Jefferson as they, still green and fresh in my memory, have occurred to me.*
>
> *I was thirty-four years old when he died. My mother was his oldest and, for the last twenty-two years of his life, his only child. She lived with him from her birth to his death, except in his absence on public service at Philadelphia and Washington. Having lost her mother at ten years [of age], she was his inseparable companion until her marriage; he had sought to supply her loss with all the watchful solicitude of a mother's tenderness. Her children were to him as the younger members of his family, having lived with him from their infancy.*
>
> *I was more intimate with him than with any man I have ever known. His character invited such intimacy—soft and feminine in his affections to his family, he entered into and sympathized with all their feelings, winning them to paths of virtue by the soothing gentleness of his manner.*

*His private apartments were open
to me at all times; I saw him under all
circumstances. While he lived, and since,
I have reviewed with severe scrutiny those
interviews, and I must say that I never
heard from him the expression of one
thought, feeling, or sentiment inconsistent
with the highest moral standard, or
the purest Christian charity in its most
enlarged sense. His moral character was of
the highest order, founded upon the purest
and sternest models of antiquity, [but]
softened, chastened, and developed by the
influences of the all pervading benevolence
of the doctrines of Christ—which he had
intensely and admiringly studied.*

*As proof of this, he left two codifications
of the morals of Jesus—one for himself,
and another for the Indians. The first of
[these] I now possess, [namely] a blank
volume, red morocco gilt, [and] lettered on
the back, "The Morals of Jesus," into which
he pasted extracts in Greek, Latin, French,
and English, taken textually from the four
Gospels, and so arranged that he could run
his eye over the readings of the same verse
in four languages.*

*The boldness and self-confidence of his
mind was the best guaranty of his*

*truthfulness. He never uttered an
untruth himself, or used duplicity, and he
condemned it in others. No end, with him,
could sanctify falsehood.*

*In his contemplative moments his
mind turned to religion, which he studied
thoroughly. He had seen and read much of
the abuses and perversions of Christianity;
he abhorred those abuses and their authors,
and denounced them without reserve. He
was regular in his attendance [at] church,
taking his prayer book with him. . . . A
gentleman of some distinction calling on
him and expressing his disbelief in the
truths of the Bible, his reply was, "Then, sir,
you have studied it to little purpose."*

*He was guilty of no profanity himself,
and did not tolerate it in others. He detested
impiety, and his favorite quotation for his
young friends, as a basis for their morals,
was the 15th psalm of David.*

*His family, by whom he was
surrounded, and who saw him in all the
unguarded privacy of private life, believed
him to be the purest of men. His precepts
were those of truth and virtue: "Be just, be
true, love your neighbor as yourself, and
your country more than yourself" were
among his favorite maxims, and they*

*recognized in him a truthful exemplar of
the precepts he taught.*

Like all holders of high office in the United
States, Jefferson had his political enemies. As an
Antifederalist, he was subjected to ongoing vilifi-
cation by the Federalist press, most of which was
originated by James Thomson Callender, a man
Jefferson pardoned as a victim of the Sedition Act.
After Callender was rejected in his effort to secure
an appointive position in the U.S. government, a
Federalist newspaper in Richmond hired him as a
journalist. Callender and his tactics were described
in the book *The Real Thomas Jefferson* as follows:

> *True to his style, [Callender] fabricated
> a series of scandalous stories about
> Jefferson's personal life, the ugliest of
> which charged him with having fathered
> several children by a mulatto slave at
> Monticello, a young woman named Sally
> Hemings.*
>
> *Although Callender had never gone
> near Jefferson's estate, he alleged that
> this was common knowledge in the
> neighboring area. He included many
> lurid details of this supposed illicit
> relationship among the "entertaining
> facts" he created for his readers, even*

*inventing the names of children whom
"Dusky Sally" had never borne.*

*Other Federalist editors took up these
accusations with glee, and Callender's
stories spread like wildfire from one end
of the country to the other—sometimes
expanded and embellished by subsequent
writers. The President was charged with
other evils as well; the torrent of slander
never seemed to let up. As one biographer
has written, "He suffered open personal
attacks which in severity and obscenity
have rarely if ever been matched in
presidential history in the United States."*

Responding to the spurious, politically inspired Sally Hemings allegations, Professor Dumas
Malone, whose six-volume biography of Jefferson
won a Pulitzer Prize, said the things Jefferson was
accused of would be "virtually unthinkable in a
man of Jefferson's moral standards and habitual
conduct." Malone went on to say,

*To say this is not to claim that he was
a plaster saint and incapable of moral
lapses. But his major weaknesses were not
of this sort. It is virtually inconceivable
that this fastidious gentleman whose
devotion to his dead wife's memory and*

*to the happiness of his daughters and
grandchildren bordered on the excessive
could have carried on through a period
of years a vulgar liaison which his own
family could not have failed to detect.
It would be as absurd as to charge this
consistently temperate man with being,
through a long period, a secret drunkard.*

When asked about the Hemings allegations, Jefferson's grandson responded by revealing that she was the mistress of Peter Carr, Jefferson's nephew, pointing out "their connection was perfectly notorious at Monticello."

Randolph shed additional light on the grandeur of his grandfather when describing the manner in which Jefferson reacted to the fraudulent attacks upon his character: "In speaking of the calumnies which his enemies had uttered against his public and private character with such unmitigated and untiring bitterness, he said that he had not considered them as abusing him; they had never known *him*. They had created an imaginary being clothed with odious attributes, to whom they had given his name; and it was against that creature of their imaginations they had leveled their anathemas."

Jefferson's character is perhaps best described in his own words: "Whenever you are to do a thing, though it can never be known but to yourself, ask yourself how you would act were all the world looking at you, and act accordingly."

That's a precept with biblical roots.

Chapter Six

John Witherspoon

Firebrand of the Revolution

A true son of liberty. So he was.
But first, he was a son of the Cross.
JOHN ADAMS'S TRIBUTE UPON LEARNING OF
JOHN WITHERSPOON'S DEATH

John Witherspoon was a conservative Christian who today would be labeled a fundamentalist. He believed, wrote, sermonized, and taught that there *are* absolutes and that the source of the knowledge of right and wrong is the Judeo-Christian Bible. He believed that God blesses and protects those individuals and nations who honor Him and that ignoring God and His precepts is a recipe for individual and national disaster. He shared these beliefs with his fellow Founders, most of whom are on record as having made similar statements.

In the subtitle of her 1976 book about Witherspoon, Martha Lou Lemmon Stohlman referred to him as "pastor, politician, and patriot," labels that accurately described the various roles he played as a Founding Father. Because of his well-known oratorical skills, Stohlman referred to Witherspoon as "a firebrand of the Revolution" and "the Big Bertha of the Popularist artillery."

Born in 1723 into a Presbyterian family in Edinburgh, Scotland, Witherspoon aligned himself, as had his father before him, with the orthodox branch of the church known as the Popularists. Witherspoon's mother was a lineal descendant of church reformer John Knox, whose Puritanical traditions the family carried on.

One of our least-known Founding Fathers, Witherspoon became a doctor of theology when he was only twenty years old. After coming to the colonies in 1768 to become president of the College of New Jersey (now known as Princeton University), Witherspoon became active in events and organizations instrumental in upholding and promoting the biblical morality of his adopted country. His reprinted sermons and political essays were widely distributed, and he is credited with playing a major role in producing a Bible thought to be America's first family Bible.

Under Witherspoon's leadership, Princeton became recognized for its biblical teaching regarding the relationship between liberty and personal responsibility. As a teacher and preacher, he believed his mission was to imprint upon the minds of his students an extensive knowledge and love of Holy Scripture. He was firm in his belief that "civil liberty cannot be long preserved without virtue."

Witherspoon promulgated a number of rules regarding student body worship, including this order: "Every student shall attend worship in the college hall morning and evening at the hours appointed and shall behave with gravity and reverence during the whole service. Every student shall attend public worship on the Sabbath."

Witherspoon's most important contribution to the formulation of the unique American system of government, moral codes, and ethical standards was to help shape the men who shaped America through his position as the college's chief lecturer, from where he touched the lives of nearly five hundred graduates. James Madison, who would later become known as the "Father of the Constitution" and would become the fourth president of the United States, was Witherspoon's most notable student. In addition to Madison, Witherspoon taught a future vice president, twenty-one future senators, twenty-nine future representatives, and fifty-six future state legislators. Of the thirty-three of Witherspoon's students who would become judges, three became members of the United States Supreme Court. More than fifty of his former students eventually became college presidents.

Many students of early American history have listed Witherspoon among such notables as Samuel Rutherford, John Locke, and William Blackstone as the most powerful and influential minds to influence the writing of the Constitution. All of them were strong believers in limited government, the rights of individuals, and freedom of personal religious beliefs. Witherspoon's direct influence upon the Constitution was also felt through the delegates to the Constitutional Convention of 1787—nearly one-sixth of the fifty-five delegates were his former students.

Most historians believe Witherspoon was the originator of the phrase "with a firm reliance on the protection of divine Providence," which is included in the last sentence of the Declaration of Independence. He was the only member of the clergy to sign that document.

Witherspoon and his fellow Popularists were inspired by John Calvin's affirmation of law and its relationship to biblical precepts. Believing there was theological authority for participation in the political arena, orthodox Presbyterians, who were closely aligned in their thinking with the

Puritans, were nearly unanimous in supporting the American Revolution.

"Witherspoon and most American political thinkers," wrote John Willson, emeritus professor of history at Hillsdale College, "believed that society was antecedent to government; that is, social institutions, rooted in the family, village life, and voluntary associations, existed prior to government and took precedent over it. In practical terms, this meant that the commanding position of Christianity in American Society would allow religion to flourish as long as the civil government did nothing to interfere with it. That Americans were a Protestant Christian people was taken for granted by Witherspoon and most of his generation."

Not one to avoid conflict, Witherspoon found himself in frequent and intense confrontations with liberal theologians who referred to themselves as the "moderate" wing of the denomination. He disdained the so-called moderates, ridiculing them in sermons and writings, including a sixty-page pamphlet entitled *Ecclesiastical Characteristics*, an excellent piece of satire published in 1763 and widely distributed in America and throughout Europe. His lengthy subtitle drips with sarcasm: *Arcana of Church Policy being an Humble Attempt to open up the Mystery of Moderation wherein is shewn a plain and easy way of attaining to the character of a* moderate man, as at present in repute in the Church of Scotland.

Another area of major concern to Witherspoon was theater, the primary source of entertainment available at that time. In his *Serious Enquiry into the Nature and Effects of the Stage*, Witherspoon wrote, "The truth is, the need of amusement is much less than most people commonly apprehend, and where it is not necessary, it must be sinful." He didn't think the expense involved to both the promoters and the public were worth it in relation to any positive effect, if any, it might have. He questioned its educational value by asking why anything needs to be known unless it leads to our spiritual improvement. Today, a vast majority of responsible people could certainly agree with his statement that "no woman. . .who has been ten times in a playhouse durst repeat in company all that she has heard there."

In a sermon delivered just prior to his election to the First Continental Congress, Witherspoon completed his remarks with this admonition:

> *Upon the whole, I beseech you to make a wise improvement of the present threatening aspect of public affairs, and to remember that your duty to God, to our country, to your families, and to yourselves, is the same. True religion is nothing else but*

*an inward temper and outward conduct
suited to your state and circumstances
in providence at any time. And as peace
with God and conformity to him, adds
to him, adds to the sweetness of created
comforts while we possess them, so in times
of difficulty and trial, it is in the man of
piety and inward principle, that we may
expect to find the uncorrupted patriot, the
useful citizen, and the invincible soldier.
God grant that in America true religion
and civil liberty may be inseparable, and
that the unjust attempts to destroy the one,
may in the issue tend to the support and
establishment of both.*

Did Reverend John Witherspoon believe in the separation of church and state? Yes, in the sense that he was absolutely opposed to the establishment of a state-controlled church. He was just as absolutely opposed to the proposition that the church had no business in the political arena. Nor would he have accepted the idea that symbols of Christianity should be hidden from public view.

Witherspoon believed freedom and religion were interdependent and said so in many of his widely reproduced sermons. As he knew from his study of history, the potential loss of political freedom, such as the colonies faced in relation to the mother country, always results in the loss of religious freedom, and he couldn't stand by idly and let that happen. "There is not a single instance in history, in which civil liberty was lost, and religious liberty preserved entire," he said.

"He is the best friend to American liberty who is the most sincere and active in promoting true and undefiled religion, and who sets himself with the greatest firmness to bear down profanity and immorality of every kind," Witherspoon said. "Whoever is an avowed enemy of God, I scruple not to call him an enemy of his country."

Prior to commencement of hostilities in the American War for Independence, Witherspoon encouraged those who would become directly involved with these words: "[T]here is no soldier so undaunted as the pious man, no army so formidable as those who are superior to the fear of death. There is nothing more awful to think of than that those whose trade is war should be despisers of the name of the Lord of hosts and that they should expose themselves to the imminent danger of being immediately sent from cursing and cruelty on earth to the blaspheming rage and despairing horror of the infernal pit. Let therefore everyone who offers himself as a champion in his country's cause be persuaded to reverence the name and walk in the fear of the Prince of the kings of the earth; and then he may with the most unshaken firmness expect the issue [God's protection] either in victory or death."

Regarding the importance of electing men or women of character to public office, Witherspoon offered this piece of advice: "Those who wish well to the State ought to choose to places of trust men of inward principle, justified by exemplary conversation. . . . Those, therefore, who pay no regard to religion and sobriety in the persons whom they send to the legislature of any State are guilty of the greatest absurdity and will soon pay dear for their folly."

Witherspoon would be astounded at the routine incivility and coarseness of today's society. "Nothing is more certain," Witherspoon said, "than that a general profligacy and corruption of manners make a people ripe for destruction. A good form of government may hold the rotten materials together for some time, but beyond a certain pitch, even the best constitution will be ineffectual, and slavery must ensue."

It is clear from the study of John Witherspoon's own words that he would be calling for revival in America today, not a diminishing of Christian influence, and certainly not a diminishing of the instillation of Christian principles in our education system. Rather than allowing the Bible to be hidden behind church doors, Witherspoon would be demanding that the Bible be restored to its rightful place of honor and authority.

Historian B. J. Lossing ended his essay on the life of Witherspoon with this fitting description:

> *As a theological writer, Doctor Witherspoon had few superiors, and as a statesman he held the first rank. In him were centered the social elements of an upright citizen, a fond parent, a just tutor, and humble Christian; and when, on the tenth of November, 1794, at the age of nearly seventy-three years, his useful life closed, it was widely felt that a "great man had fallen in Israel."*

Chapter Seven

James Madison

Father of the Constitution

We have all been encouraged to feel in the guardianship and guidance of that Almighty Being, whose power regulates the destiny of nations.
JAMES MADISON

At the young age of twenty-three, James Madison was already committed to independence from Great Britain and to the formation of a republican form of government in America. Often referred to as the Father of the Constitution, he has been acclaimed by his biographers for his energy, his determination, his character, and his deep-seated devotion to the principle of religious freedom and the individual liberties associated with it.

While serving as a member of the Constitutional Convention of 1787, Madison spoke more than 160 times, helping to keep the oftentimes contentious proceedings from getting hopelessly bogged down. He is said to have been the best prepared of the Convention delegates, arriving in Philadelphia well ahead of its scheduled opening date armed with ideas gleaned from his extensive studies of confederacies. According to William Pierce, delegate from Georgia, Madison possessed "the most correct knowledge [of] the affairs of the United States" to be found among the political leaders of his generation.

Described as "an indefatigable reporter," Madison is credited with keeping the most detailed and reliable records of the convention's proceedings. "I chose a seat in front of the presiding member, with the other members on my right and left hand," Madison later wrote. "In this favorable position for hearing all that passed, I noted in terms legible and in abbreviations and marks intelligible to myself what was read from the Chair or spoken by the members; and losing not a moment unnecessarily between the adjournment and reassembling of the Convention I was enabled to write out my daily notes during the session or within a few finishing days after its close in the extent and form preserved in my own hand on my files. I was not absent a single day, nor more than a fraction of an hour in any day, so that I could not have lost a single speech unless a very short one."

Without Madison's journal, many interesting and informative details of the proceedings leading to the writing of the U.S. Constitution would be left to conjecture. In reference to Madison's Convention journal, Thomas Jefferson stated in a letter to John Adams in 1815, "Do you know that there exists in manuscript the ablest work of this kind ever yet executed, of the debates of the constitutional convention of Philadelphia? The whole of everything said and done there was taken down by Mr. Madison, with a labor and exactness beyond comprehension."

While not necessarily known as outspoken regarding his Christianity, Madison made the motion that the Convention delegates accept Benjamin Franklin's appeal for prayer, a motion seconded by Roger Sherman. Later, Madison acknowledged his conviction that God had directed the outcome: "It is impossible for the man of pious reflection not to perceive in the [Constitutional] Convention a finger of that Almighty hand."

Many historians have highlighted Madison's role as the Founder most responsible for the eventual addition of the Bill of Rights to the U.S. Constitution. In 1776, Madison, as a delegate to the Virginia Constitutional Convention, had worked closely with Jefferson on the committee that prepared a declaration of individual rights. Madison's having written the Virginia provision that asserted the right "to the free exercise of religion, according to the dictates of conscience" was a foreshadowing of his later efforts to add a Bill of Rights to the new U.S. Constitution. More to the point, he said, "Religion [is] the basis and Foundation of Government." Madison is also credited with authoring this specific clause: "Congress shall make no law respecting an establishment of religion, *or prohibiting the free exercise thereof.*"

Getting the Bill of Rights approved wasn't an easy task, largely due to the fact that a majority of delegates to the Constitutional Convention at first concluded a list of individual rights wasn't necessary because of the limited nature of the proposed federal government. The Federalists' position was that the people retained all powers not specifically delegated to the federal government by the proposed Constitution. The anti-Federalists rejected this logic as wishful thinking. Little by little, they made their case. Jefferson lent his support, saying, "No just government should refuse, or rest on inference." Speaking a little more bluntly, Madison was quoted as saying, "All men having power ought to be distrusted to a certain degree."

It soon became obvious that without a bill of rights, ratification of the Constitution would face stiff, perhaps lethal, opposition; Rhode Island and

North Carolina refused to ratify the Constitution specifically because it didn't include a specific list of individual rights. Other states held back their support for that and other reasons. A compromise in Massachusetts allowed the ratification process to go forward in 1788 with the understanding that a proposed list of amendments would be considered by the new Congress. In 1791, ten amendments, known as the Bill of Rights, were approved by Congress and became part of the Constitution.

To help generate support for ratification, Madison, along with Alexander Hamilton and John Jay, authored a series of eighty-five articles, many under the signature of Publius, known as *The Federalist*. Madison is believed to have authored twenty-six of the articles, which were printed by a large number of influential newspapers.

With the Bill of Rights in place, Madison became comfortable with Federalist demands for a strong national defense, a coherent national foreign policy, and issues connected with international trade. Tax collection and payment of public debt could only be enforced, he realized, through a federal government. "The powers delegated by the proposed Constitution to the federal government," Madison said, "are few and defined [and] will be exercised principally on external objects, such as war, peace, negotiation and foreign commerce."

Madison also advocated the development of uniform rules and regulations among the states to govern trade and interstate commercial relations. That's because he was convinced that only a federal government, albeit with divided and balanced powers, would be able to effectively enforce such regulations. He argued that "the people would not be less free as members of one great Republic than as members of thirteen small ones." Although convinced of the need for a stronger federal government, Madison, because of his dedication to individual freedom, retained an anti-Federalist side to his thinking. Some historians have described Madison's form of Federalism as a "mild" form.

"In framing a government which is to be administered by men over men, the great difficulty lies in this: you must first enable the government to control the governed; and in the next place oblige it to control itself," Madison wrote. Many of his writings in *The Federalist* emphasized that the Constitution "leaves to the several States a residuary and inviolable sovereignty over all other objects," referring to the fact that the new federal government had superior authority over "certain enumerated objects only." Later, his move back toward anti-Federalist thinking led to his friendship with Jefferson.

When Jefferson was elected president in 1801, he appointed Madison Secretary of State. In that capacity, and as a result of their growing friendship, Madison became the president's most trusted advisor. Upon Jefferson's retirement at the end of his second term as president, Madison defeated Federalist candidate Charles Cotesworth Pinckney of South Carolina to become America's fourth president. On March 4, 1809, United States Chief Justice John Marshall swore Madison into office.

Madison was born March 16, 1751, in Port Conway, Virginia, where he was raised by devout Episcopalian parents. At that time, the Episcopal/Anglican Church was the state-sanctioned church of Virginia. Harshness of the church in dealing with dissidents had helped to form his staunch support for religious freedom.

Madison was educated at home by his mother, grandmother, and tutors, from whom he received a classical and spiritually based preparatory education prior to his enrolling in the College of New Jersey, soon to become Princeton University.

Originally a divinity student, Madison was substantially influenced by Reverend John Witherspoon, a prominent theologian and legal scholar as well as president of the college. His advanced education under the Christian patriot Witherspoon provided Madison with a lifelong theological orientation and understanding of history and law that helped to motivate him to focus his legislative activities on the protection of individual rights.

At the age of forty-three, Madison married Dolley Payne Todd, a widow and committed Christian who reportedly shared his knowledge of Scripture.

That Madison was a devout Christian who believed in God's involvement in the founding of America cannot be denied. "No people," he said, "ought to feel greater obligations to celebrate the goodness of the Great Disposer of Events and of the Destiny of Nations than the people of the United States. And to the same Divine Author of every good and perfect gift we are indebted for all those privileges and advantages, religious as well as civil, which are so richly enjoyed in this favored land."

That "Divine Author," his contemporaries knew, was the Judeo-Christian God to whom all men are accountable. "Before any man can be considered as a member of civil society," Madison pointed out, "he must be considered as a subject of the Governor of the Universe."

"The belief in a God All Powerful wise and good, is so essential to the moral order of the world and to the happiness of man, that arguments which enforce it cannot be drawn from too many sources nor adapted with too much solicitude to the different characters and capacities impressed with it," Madison said.

It is clear from Madison's own words and the

words of the other Founders that they never intended for the Christian religion to be walled off from the government they founded. Nor did they intend for judges to usurp the legislative process.

Madison had this to say regarding the intended power of the Legislative Branch (Congress) versus the Judiciary (the courts): "The members of the legislative department are numerous. They are distributed and dwell among the people at large. Their connections of blood, or friendship, and of acquaintance embrace a great proportion of the most influential part of the society. They are more immediately the confidential guardians of the rights and liberties of the people."

Sir William Blackstone, author of *Commentaries on the Laws of England*, and the legal scholar most often quoted by the Founding Fathers where the judiciary was concerned, wrote: "If [the legislature] will positively enact a thing to be done, the judges are not at liberty to reject it, for that were to set the judicial power above that of the legislature, which would be subversive of all government." (Blackstone's *Commentaries* provided the foundation of legal education in America.)

Echoing that sentiment, the Father of the Constitution said, "I beg to know upon what principle it can be contended that any one department draws from the Constitution greater powers than another. I do not see that any one of these independent departments has more right than another to declare their sentiments on that point."

Although small in stature, James Madison was a giant in the deliberations and events that led to creation and ratification of the U.S. Constitution, a unique document in the history of the world. He died on July 4, 1836, outliving all the other Founding Fathers.

Chapter Eight

Roger Sherman

Master Builder of the Constitution

. . .an old Puritan, as honest as an angel
and as firm in the cause of American
Independence as Mount Atlas.
ROGER SHERMAN AS DESCRIBED
BY JOHN ADAMS

A friend of Roger Sherman once described him as "twistical," no doubt based upon Sherman's reputation as a skillful legislator. His friend Jeremiah Wadsworth apparently was referring to Sherman's generally recognized ability during his many years of holding elective office to maneuver his way through the twists and turns of political give-and-take in order to accomplish his goals; Wadsworth said Sherman was "cunning as the devil."

Historians have cited Sherman as one of the most effective members of the Constitutional Convention in moving the delegates to the successful completion of what has often been recognized as the "Miracle of Philadelphia." Although he had serious reservations regarding the idea of establishing a strong national government by scrapping the Articles of Confederation, Sherman—along with George Washington, Alexander Hamilton, Charles Cotesworth Pinckney, and James Madison—was eventually recognized as a "master builder of the Constitution."

Sherman, senior in age to every delegate to the Philadelphia Convention except Benjamin Franklin, was the only Founding Father to sign all four of what are considered America's major founding documents: The Articles of Association in 1774, the Declaration of Independence in 1776, the Articles of Confederation in 1777, and the United States Constitution in 1787. Sherman's signature on the Articles of Association established him as one of the more prominent Founding Fathers.

The transformation from a group of loosely associated colonies to a united entity that would eventually become the United States of America took a great leap forward when the First Continental Congress produced the Articles of Association in 1774. Although they were a forerunner to the

Declaration of Independence, the threat of rebellion was not mentioned in the Articles. That message to King George, which many believe *did* set the colonies on the road to revolution, was intended only as a petition of grievances in response to the "Intolerable Acts" British Parliament had imposed on the colonies. Among other things, the grievances specifically mentioned were: the deprivation of the right to a jury trial; the prosecution in England for crimes committed in America; and the various penalizing acts specifically targeted upon the citizens of Boston and the Massachusetts Bay Colony as a whole. The most egregious of those acts was the Massachusetts Government Act, which nullified all colonial control over their own government and courts.

The Articles led to a boycott of some British goods, which only brought on other retaliatory acts by Parliament. Predictably, that created more discontent among the colonists. Although few were immediately ready for a final break, the downward spiral in British-American relations was gaining momentum.

While Sherman was strongly opposed to the punitive acts Parliament had designed to punish the colonies following the Boston Tea Party, he was slow to accept the idea of *armed* resistance. The occupation of Massachusetts by British troops and the passage of the Intolerable Acts were the deciding factors in putting Sherman firmly on the side of rebellion. Later, in recognition of his legislative abilities and common sense, he was selected as a member of the separate committees that produced both the Declaration of Independence and the Articles of Confederation. But many historians believe his single most important contribution to U.S. history was the important role he played as a delegate to the Constitutional Convention.

Although Sherman had serious differences with the Federalists, he understood that the United States of America could not be united in name only. The former colonies were becoming an important member of the international community, and as such they could only operate successfully as one united country rather than as a loose association of individual sovereign states, any of which could go their own way regarding selected issues. The states had to speak with one voice in foreign policy and in matters related to international trade, which they could not do absent a national government. National defense required an effective military establishment; the states had to have a method of raising money through taxation in order to support the military and other critical needs. The delegates eventually agreed that there had to be a responsible entity—that is, a national treasury— that could establish the new nation's financial creditability, and that there had to be a federal agency with the means and authority to pay the country's bills.

Sherman, though, was adamant in his belief that it would not be acceptable for a federal government to interfere with the government of individual states nor with the rights of individuals. He was instrumental in preventing a provision that would have allowed the federal government to have veto power over state laws.

Sherman is well remembered for proposing the Connecticut Plan. Also known as the Great Compromise, and sometimes as the Sherman Compromise, the plan opened the way toward America's bicameral legislature, under which each state would have equal representation in the U.S. Senate (two senators from each state) and proportional representation (based on each state's population) in the U.S. House of Representatives.

That highly emotional issue had threatened to bring the Convention to an unsuccessful conclusion; feeling the situation was hopeless, some delegates had already left Philadelphia. During a lengthy speech delivered at the height of the tension, Benjamin Franklin said, "We are sent here to consult, not to contend with each other; and declarations of a fixed opinion, and of determined resolution never to change it, neither enlighten nor convince us. Positiveness and warmth on one side naturally beget their like on the other; and tend to create and augment discord and division in a great concern, wherein harmony and union are extremely necessary to give weight to our councils, and render them effectual in promoting and securing the common good."

When Franklin had finished speaking, calm was restored and the delegates moved forward to finish the business at hand. Sherman's name had been linked with Franklin's earlier during the Convention, when he seconded Franklin's motion to open each day of the Constitutional Convention with prayer.

Once the Constitution was put into final form and approved by the delegates, the next hurdle was to get at least nine of the thirteen states to ratify it. Sherman was instrumental in securing ratification by the influential state of Connecticut.

Although Sherman had little formal education, the well-educated John Adams said of him, "Destitute of all literary and scientific education, but such as he acquired by his own exertions, he was one of the most sensible men in the world. The clearest head and steadiest heart." Such tributes were common among those who knew Sherman well. The Rev. Ezra Stiles, a Congregational minister and president of Yale College, said Sherman "had that Dignity which arises from doing every Thing perfectly right. He was an extraordinary

Man—a venerable uncorrupted Patriot."

Growing up in a Congregationalist church whose doctrines were rooted in English Puritanism, Sherman believed that piety and sound morals were two pillars necessary to good individual citizenship and that it is therefore altogether proper for the state to disseminate religious truth. At the same time, he was opposed to any kind of state control over the church. That attitude of cooperation/separation between church and state was generally accepted by his fellow Founding Fathers.

Sherman's writings reflect his strong commitment to the Christian faith as illustrated by the revised creed he wrote for the White Haven Congregational Church:

> *I believe that there is one only living*
> *and true God, existing In three persons,*
> *the Father, the Son, and the Holy Ghost,*
> *the same in substance equal in power and*
> *glory. That the scriptures of the old and new*
> *testaments are a revelation from God and*
> *a complete rule to direct us how we may*
> *glorify and enjoy him.*
>
> *That God has foreordained whatsoever*
> *comes to pass, so as thereby he is not the*
> *author or approver of sin.*
>
> *That he creates all things, and preserves*
> *and governs all creatures and all their*

actions, in a manner perfectly consistent with the freedom of will in moral agents, and the usefulness of means.

That he made man at first perfectly holy, that the first man sinned, and as he was the public head of his posterity, they all became sinners in consequence of his first transgression, are wholly indisposed to that which is good and inclined to evil, and on account of sin are liable to all the miseries of this life, to death, and to the pains of hell forever.

I believe that God having elected some of mankind to eternal life, did send his own Son to become man, die in the room and stead of sinners and thus to lay a foundation for the offer of pardon and salvation to all mankind, so as all may be saved who are willing to accept the gospel offer:

Also by his special grace and spirit, to regenerate, sanctify and enable to persevere in holiness, all who shall be saved; and to procure in consequence of their repentance and faith in himself their justification by virtue of his atonement as the only meritorious cause.

I believe a visible church to be a congregation of those who make a credible

*profession of their faith in Christ, and
obedience to him, joined by the bond of the
covenant. . . .*

*I believe that the souls of believers are
at their death made perfectly holy, and
immediately taken to glory: that at the end
of this world there will be a resurrection
of the dead, and a final judgment of all
mankind, when the righteous shall be
publicly acquitted by Christ the Judge and
admitted to everlasting life and glory, and
the wicked be sentenced to everlasting
punishment.*

On Friday, September 25, 1789, the day after
the U.S. House of Representatives approved the
First Amendment to the Constitution, New Jersey Representative Elias Boudinot proposed that
Congress should request that President George
Washington issue a Thanksgiving proclamation
for "the many signal favors of Almighty God." In
his proposal, Boudinot made specific mention of
Sherman's influence on Congress. The resolution
reads as follows:

> *Resolved, That a joint committee of
> both Houses be directed to wait upon
> the President of the United States to
> request that he would recommend to*

*the people of the United States a day of
public thanksgiving and prayer, to be
observed by acknowledging with grateful
hearts the many signal favors of Almighty
God, especially by affording them an
opportunity peaceable to establish a
Constitution of government for their
safety and happiness. . . .*

*Mr. [Roger] Sherman justified the
practice of thanksgiving, on any signal
event, not only as a laudable one in
itself but as warranted by a number of
precedents in Holy Writ for instance,
the solemn thanksgivings and rejoicings
which took place in the time of Solomon
after the building of the temple was a case
in point. This example he thought worthy
of Christian imitation on the present
occasion; and he would agree with the
gentleman who moved the resolution.
Mr. Boudinot quoted further precedents
from the practice of the last Congress and
hoped the motion would meet a ready
acquiescence [approval]. The question
was not put on the resolution and it was
carried in the affirmative.*

President Washington approved the Congressional resolution and issued the Thanksgiving

Proclamation on October 3, 1789.

In life and in death, Sherman bore witness to his strong and active Christian faith. His life was a testimony to the important role Christians and the Bible played in the formation of America's systems of government and commerce.

Chapter Nine

George Mason
Father of the Bill of Rights

*The laws of nature are the laws of God,
whose authority can be superseded by no
power on earth. (Later included in the
Declaration of Independence as "the laws
of nature and nature's God.")*
GEORGE MASON

Although George Mason had strong convictions regarding his vision for the new Republic he helped to establish, he harbored no ambitions where national political offices were concerned, preferring the quiet life in his beloved Gunston Hall estate in Virginia to a high profile political career in the new government. Although highly esteemed by his contemporaries—Thomas Jefferson referred to Mason as "the wisest man of his generation," and James Madison called him "the greatest debater" he ever knew—George Mason nevertheless seems to have been pushed into the shadows of early American history.

Mason was the primary author of one of the more important but lesser known anti-British documents the colonists produced, the *Fairfax Resolves*. It was adopted on July 8, 1774, at Mount Vernon, Virginia, during a convention George Washington chaired. The resolution was an unambiguous statement of colonial rights and a revolutionary call for the colonies to organize in protesting British Parliament's actions following the Boston Tea Party.

Article One of the *Resolves* stated that "this Colony and Dominion of Virginia can not be considered as a conquered Country; and if it was, that the present Inhabitants are the Descendants not of the Conquered, but of the Conquerors." In other words, the colonists demanded their right to be treated as fellow citizens rather than a foreign country recently placed under British control. Issues specifically mentioned included Colonial representation in Parliament, especially where taxation was concerned, control over military forces located within the colonies, judicial independence, and less British interference in commercial activities and policies. Unspecified actions to enforce American rights were strongly implied. In this document, the Colonials served notice that they, while loyal subjects, were not going to be treated as second-class citizens and that independence was an option.

Mason was outspokenly anti-Federalist in that he did not trust in the basic concept of a strong central government. But he did understand that the fledgling nation he was helping to establish had to speak with one voice in its dealings with other nations. And that voice, he understood, had to have substance behind it. That substance could only be created and wielded effectively by a central government, one that had the power to "raise taxes and wage war."

Eventually becoming a lukewarm supporter of the Federalist cause, Mason remained quite concerned with maintaining states' rights: "The State Legislatures," he warned, "ought to have some means of defending themselves against encroachments of the National Government." Mason also articulated his desire that the states be protected from the possibility of tyranny by federal courts.

Mason was unabashedly opposed to the institution of slavery: "Every master of slaves is born a petty tyrant," he said. "They bring the judgment of heaven upon a country. As nations cannot be rewarded or punished in the next world, they must be in this. By an inevitable chain of causes and effects, Providence punishes national sins, by national calamities."

Mason is said to have influenced Thomas Jefferson in drafting the Northwest Ordinance, which included a prohibition against slavery in the new states. "As much as I value a union of all the States," Mason said, "I would not admit the Southern States into the Union unless they agree to the discontinuance of this disgraceful trade."

Even though Mason owned more than two hundred slaves himself, he was on record as saying he wanted to see all slaves freed. Like most of the northern delegates to the Constitutional Convention, he was opposed to the *concept* of forced slavery, but he understood the necessity that the slavery issue, as important as it was, be subordinate to the finalization of a constitution that could be ratified. The Ship of State had to be launched, shaken down, and securely afloat before other important issues could be addressed. The men charged with that difficult task understood the realities of the times: They had to make distasteful compromises to accomplish their main goal.

In his excellent explanation of the dilemma with which the convention delegates were faced, well-known historian, author, and lecturer Paul Johnson wrote:

In August the Convention turned its attention to the knotty problem of slavery, which produced the second major compromise [of the convention]. The debating was complex, not to say convoluted, since Mason, the biggest slave-holder attending, attacked the institution and especially the slave trade. Article I, section 9, grants Congress the power to regulate or ban the slave trade as of January 1, 1808. On slavery itself the Northerners were prepared to compromise because they knew they had no alternative. Indeed, as one historian of slavery has put it, "It would have been impossible to establish a national government in the 18th century [in America] without recognizing slavery in some way." The convention did this in three respects. First, it omitted any condemnation of slavery. Second, it adopted Madison's three-fifths rule, which gave the slave states the added power of counting the slaves as voters, on the basis that each slave counted as three-fifths of a freeman, while of course refusing them the vote as such—a masterly piece of humbug in itself. Third, the words "slave" and "slavery" were deliberately avoided

> in the text. As Madison himself said (on
> August 25), it would be wrong "to admit
> in the Constitution the idea that there
> could be property in men."

Mason, described by some as "a flaming patriot," was said to be a "man of the people" because of his dedication to including a guarantee of individual rights in the Constitution. Mason and all his fellow Founders, having been born and raised under the protections of the English Bill of Rights of 1689, were determined to preserve individual rights, even though separating from the mother country. Often referred to as the "Father of the Bill of Rights," Mason is credited with producing the first ten amendments to the Constitution, which specifically address those rights. Earlier, he had written the Virginia Declaration of Rights included in his home state's Constitution that said:

> A declaration of rights made by the
> Representatives of the good people of
> Virginia, assembled in full and free
> Convention; which rights do pertain to
> them and their posterity, as the basis and
> foundation of government.
> That all men are by nature equally
> free and independent, and have certain
> inherent rights, of which, when they

enter into a state of society, they cannot, by any compact, deprive or divest their posterity; namely, the enjoyment of life and liberty, with the means of acquiring and possessing property, and pursuing and obtaining happiness and safety.

That all power is vested in, and consequently derived from, the People; that magistrates are their trustees and servants, and at all times amenable to them.

That government is, or ought to be, instituted for the common benefit, protection, and security of the people, nation, or community—of all the various modes and forms of Government that is best which is capable of producing the greatest degree of happiness and safety, and is most effectually secured against the danger of mal-administration;—and that, whenever any Government shall be found inadequate or contrary to these purposes, a majority of the community hath an indubitable, unalienable, and indefeasible right, to reform, alter, or abolish it, in such manner as shall be judged most conducive to the publick weal.

That no man, or set of men, are entitled to exclusive or separate

*emoluments and privileges from the
community, but in consideration of
publick services; which, not being
descendible, neither ought the offices of
Magistrate, Legislator, or Judge, to be
hereditary.*

*That no free Government, or the
blessing of liberty, can be preserved to any
people but by a firm adherence to justice,
moderation, temperance, frugality, and
virtue, and by frequent recurrence to
fundamental principles.*

*That Religion, or the duty which we
owe to our Creator, and the manner
of discharging it, can be directed only
by reason and conviction, not by force
or violence; and, therefore, all men are
equally entitled to the free exercise of
religion, according to the dictates of
conscience; and that it is the mutual duty
of all to practice Christian forbearance,
love, and charity, towards each other.*

James Mason believed that the House of Representatives should be the most powerful part of
the federal government because the composition
of the House is determined by each state's population. His worst fear was that the federal government would someday trample states' rights.

Mason seems to have been envisioning the likelihood of judges meddling in the realm reserved for the legislative branch of government with this ominous observation: "When we reflect upon the insidious art of wicked and designing men, the various and plausible pretenses for continuing and increasing the inordinate lust of power in the few, we shall no longer be surprised that freeborn man hath been enslaved, and those very means which were contrived for his preservation [such as the First Amendment] have been perverted to his ruin."

Those who are confused regarding the Founders' original intent regarding the controversy over "separation of church and state" should think about this sentiment expressed by Mason and echoed by most of the Founding Fathers: "All men have an equal, natural and unalienable right to the free exercise of religion, according to the dictates of conscience; and that no particular sect or society of Christianity ought to be favored or established by law in preference to others."

In other words, there was to be no officially sanctioned Christian denomination but the government has no right to interfere with the "the free exercise of religion." That individual right means the government—including the judicial branch, which obviously is part of the federal government—is to have *no* control over anyone's right to participate in or extol their religion either publicly or privately.

At the end of the Constitutional Convention, Mason refused to add his signature to the document because he believed that it gave the federal government too much power at the expense of the individual states. The power given to the federal judiciary was a specific issue with which he strongly disagreed.

Eventually, the required nine states, including Mason's home state of Virginia, ratified the Constitution. "We are now to rank among the nations of the world," Mason said, "but whether our Independence shall prove a blessing or a curse must depend upon our own wisdom or folly, virtue or wickedness. . . . Justice and virtue are the vital principles of republican government."

Mason was born in Fairfax County, Virginia, in 1725, and he died there in 1792. A member of the Anglican Church, he, along with George Washington, was a vestryman of Truro Parish. In his last will and testament, Mason left no doubt regarding his Christian beliefs:

> *I, George Mason, of "Gunston Hall," in the parish of Truro and county of Fairfax, being of perfect and sound mind and memory and in good health, but mindful*

of the uncertainty of human life and the imprudence of man's leaving his affairs to be settled upon a deathbed, do make and appoint this my last Will and Testament.

My soul, I resign into the hands of my Almighty Creator, whose tender mercies are over all His works, who hateth nothing that He hath made and to the Justice and Wisdom of whose dispensation I willing and cheerfully submit, humbly hoping from His unbounded mercy and benevolence, through the merits of my blessed Savior, a remission of my sins.

Chapter Ten

John Jay

Father of American Conservatism

*Providence has given to our people the choice
of their rulers, and it is the duty, as well as
the privilege and interest of our Christian
nation to select and prefer Christians for
their rulers.*
JOHN JAY, FIRST CHIEF JUSTICE
OF THE UNITED STATES

Like his friend George Washington, John Jay spoke
and wrote frequently regarding his belief that a free
and independent United States of America was
providentially assured. Jay also shared Washington's belief that manners, morality, and virtue had
to be cultivated as part of the national character in
order for the country, and individuals, to remain in

God's good graces.

"Let a general reformation of manners take place—let universal charity, public spirit, and private virtue be inculcated, encouraged, and practiced," Jay said. "Unite in preparing for a vigorous defence of your country, as if all depended on your own exertions. And when you have done all things, then rely upon the good Providence of Almighty God for success, in full confidence that without his blessings, all our efforts will inevitably fail."

Jay was among those who were slow to accept the idea that war with Great Britain was inevitable. Conservative in nature, well-mannered, and somewhat reserved in his rhetoric, he was highly respected by his fellow members of Congress. Some historians have called him "the father of American conservatism."

After serving as a member of the First Continental Congress, Jay was selected as a delegate to the Second Continental Congress, which produced the Olive Branch Petition, a last-ditch effort in 1775 to avoid all-out war with the British. Even though the Battles of Lexington and Concord had already been fought and the American militia had surrounded Boston, Congress decided to make one more attempt at reconciliation. Considering the situation, the petition was couched in remarkably conciliatory, some might say self-demeaning, language:

To the King's Most Excellent Majesty.
MOST GRACIOUS SOVEREIGN:
We, your Majesty's faithful subjects
of the Colonies of New-Hampshire,
Massachusetts-Bay, Rhode-Island, New-
Jersey, Pennsylvania, the Counties of
Newcastle, Kent, and Sussex, on Delaware,
Maryland, Virginia, North Carolina, and
South Carolina, in behalf of ourselves
and the inhabitants of these Colonies,
who have deputed us to represent them in
General Congress, entreat your Majesty's
gracious attention to this our humble
petition.

The union between our Mother
Country and these Colonies, and the
energy of mild and just Government,
produce benefits so remarkably important,
and afforded such an assurance of their
permanency and increase, that the wonder
and envy of other nations were excited,
while they beheld Great Britain rising to a
power the most extra-ordinary the world
had ever known.

The petition went on to respectfully itemize the many colonial grievances and appealed for relief in the hope that reason could override emotions heating up on both sides. Maintaining its deferential parlance, the petition concluded:

> *We therefore beseech your Majesty,*
> *that your royal authority and influence*
> *may be graciously interposed to procure*
> *us relief from our afflicting fears and*
> *jealousies, occasioned by the system*
> *before-mentioned, and to settle peace*
> *through every part of our Dominions,*
> *with all humility submitting to your*
> *Majesty's wise consideration, whether*
> *it may not be expedient, for facilitating*
> *those important purposes, that your*
> *Majesty be pleased to direct some mode,*
> *by which the united applications of*
> *your faithful Colonists to the Throne,*
> *in pursuance of their common counsels,*
> *may be improved into a happy and*
> *permanent reconciliation; and that, in*
> *the mean time, measures may be taken*
> *for preventing the further destruction of*
> *the lives of your Majesty's subjects; and*
> *that such statutes as more immediately*
> *distress any of your Majesty's Colonies*
> *may be repealed.*
>
> *For such arrangements as your*
> *Majesty's wisdom can form for collecting*
> *the united sense of your American*

people, we are convinced your Majesty would receive such satisfactory proofs of the disposition of the Colonists towards their Sovereign and Parent State, that the wished for opportunity would soon be restored to them, of evincing the sincerity of their professions, by every testimony of devotion becoming the most dutiful subjects, and the most affectionate Colonists.

That your Majesty may enjoy long und prosperous reign, and that your descendants may govern your Dominions with honour to themselves and happiness to their subjects, is our sincere prayer.

Shortly following delivery of the Olive Branch Petition to King George, the Continental Congress produced another, much less conciliatory document entitled a *Declaration of the causes and necessity for taking up arms.* It began with this rebuke:

If it was possible for men, who exercise their reason to believe, that the divine Author of our existence intended a part of the human race to hold an absolute property in, and an unbounded power over others, marked out by his infinite

*goodness and wisdom, as the objects
of a legal domination never rightfully
resistible, however severe and oppressive,
the inhabitants of these colonies might at
least require from the parliament of Great-
Britain some evidence, that this dreadful
authority over them, has been granted to
that body. But a reverence for our great
Creator, principles of humanity, and the
dictates of common sense, must convince
all those who reflect upon the subject, that
government was instituted to promote
the welfare of mankind, and ought to be
administered for the attainment of that
end.*

The Declaration continued to lay out the Colonies' case and ended with these stern words:

*Our cause is just. Our union is perfect.
Our internal resources are great,
and, if necessary, foreign assistance is
undoubtably attainable—we gratefully
acknowledge, as signal instances of
the Divine favour towards us, that his
Providence would not permit us to
be called into this severe controversy,
until we were grown up to our present
strength, had been previously exercised*

in warlike operation, and possessed of the means of defending ourselves. With hearts fortified with these animating reflections, we most solemnly, before God and the world, declare, that exerting the utmost energy of those powers, which our beneficent Creator hath graciously bestowed upon us, the arms we have been compelled by our enemies to assume, we will, in defiance of every hazard, with unabating firmness and perseverance, employ for the preservation of our liberties; being with one mind resolved to die freemen rather than to live slaves.

In our own native land, in defence of the freedom that is our birthright, and which we ever enjoyed till the late violation of it—for the protection of our property, acquired solely by the honest industry of our fore-fathers and ourselves, against violence actually offered, we have taken up arms. We shall lay them down when hostilities shall cease on the part of the aggressors, and all danger of their being renewed shall be removed, and not before.

With an humble confidence in the mercies of the supreme and impartial

> *Judge and Ruler of the Universe, we most*
> *devoutly implore his divine goodness*
> *to protect us happily through this great*
> *conflict, to dispose our adversaries to*
> *reconciliation on reasonable terms, and*
> *thereby to relieve the empire from the*
> *calamities of civil war.*

The British king ignored the colonists' efforts to avoid war and declared them to be in a state of rebellion. A few months later, he issued a proclamation forbidding any commerce between Britain and the United States. At that point, those colonists favoring independence were leading the parade, although there were still many who favored making further efforts toward reconciliation.

Recognized at the young age of thirty-one for his wisdom and clear thinking, Jay was given a major role in drafting the first constitution of the state of New York, where he also served as Chief Justice of the state Supreme Court during the War for Independence. In 1779, he was selected to serve as a roving ambassador to several European capitals with the purpose of securing allies and funding for the revolution. Jay, Benjamin Franklin, Thomas Jefferson, John Adams, and Henry Laurens represented the United States in the peace negotiations that produced the 1783 Treaty of Paris, which officially ended the Revolutionary War. It was according to terms of the Paris treaty that Great Britain officially recognized the American colonies as a free and sovereign country.

Jay returned from Europe in 1784, at which time he was appointed Secretary of State, then known as Secretary of Foreign Affairs, a position he held for five years. It was while serving in this office that he became acutely aware of the shortcomings of the Articles of Confederation, especially where America's international interests were concerned. Jay became an early advocate of generating a new constitution rather than revamping the Articles of Confederation. He is credited with helping Alexander Hamilton found the Federalist Party.

Hamilton, Jay, and James Madison combined to author *The Federalist*, a series of eighty-five essays published between October of 1787 and April of 1788 that effectively explained the advantages of replacing the Articles. Originally published in New York newspapers, *The Federalist Papers* were instrumental in gaining support for the new Constitution.

On June 21, 1788, New Hampshire became the ninth state to ratify the Constitution, thereby officially putting it into effect. On March 4, 1789, Congress agreed that government would begin to operate under the Constitution, and on April 30, 1789, George Washington was inaugurated as the first president of the United States. In forming his administration, Washington gave Jay his choice of two positions, Secretary of State or Chief Justice of the first Supreme Court. Jay chose the latter.

In 1794 Washington entrusted Jay with handling the national task for which he is best remembered: a treaty with Great Britain that became known as "Jay's Treaty." The primary benefit of Jay's negotiations on behalf of the United States was avoiding becoming involved in a looming war between France and England, which Washington thought could be disastrous. Although the treaty was highly controversial, Washington felt that it had accomplished its purposes and agreed with Jay's assessment that "to do more was not possible." As a result of the controversy, the movement toward formation of two opposing political parties in America rapidly gained momentum.

Upon his return to the United States, Jay learned he had been elected governor of his home state of New York. He served two terms, from 1795 to 1801, and then retired from public service. In 1818, he was elected president of the Westchester Bible Society; three years later, he was elected president of the American Bible Society. "The Bible," Jay said, "is the best of all books, for it is the word of God and teaches us the way to be happy in this world and in the next."

While Jay was adamantly opposed to any state

involvement in religious matters, he believed the establishment of a free and independent United States of America had been ordained in heaven to be a Christian nation and that America was a nation of destiny, especially in proclaiming and spreading the Christian religion.

Born December 12, 1745, in New York City into an orthodox Protestant family, Jay was home-schooled. He learned Latin at the age of eight prior to attending grammar school in New Rochelle. At the age of fourteen, he enrolled in King's College, now Columbia University.

Jay died May 17, 1829, a confident and fulfilled man, leaving this statement as part of his last will and testament:

> *Unto Him who is the author and*
> *giver of all good, I render sincere and*
> *humble thanks for His manifold and*
> *unmerited blessings, and especially for*
> *our redemption and salvation by His*
> *beloved Son. He has been pleased to*
> *bless me with excellent parents, with a*
> *virtuous wife, and with worthy children.*
> *His protection has accompanied me*
> *through many eventful years, faithfully*
> *employed in the service of my country;*
> *and his providence has not only*

conducted me to this tranquil situation,
but also given me abundant reason to be
contented and thankful. Blessed be His
holy name. While my children lament
my departure, let them recollect that in
doing them good, I was only the agent of
their Heavenly Father, and that he never
withdraws his care and consolations
from those who diligently seek him.

Chapter Eleven

Benjamin Franklin
The First American

Without virtue man can have no happiness.
BENJAMIN FRANKLIN

Because of his prominence in so many various fields of endeavor, Franklin has been labeled by some as "the first American." He excelled as a scientist, inventor, author, publisher, philosopher, diplomat, and master political theorist.

In his book *Humorists*, historian and author Paul Johnson explained the reason behind that label:

> *During his lifetime the American character emerged with a flourish: as colonial Americans fought their way to independence, they drew up the first*

*successful republican constitution, and put
it to work in so thorough a manner that it
has lasted to this day—suitably amended,
of course. Franklin was the original can-
do American, to whom nothing was
impossible. He was also the first American
humorist. He invented American humor,
and many of its devices, including the one-
liner. Moreover he invented the national
mood in which American humor has
flourished: that the world is a good and
cheerful place, and everyone has an equal
right to be happy in it. If you're not happy,
Franklin argued, then very probably there
is something the matter with you, not the
world.*

"He also revealed dispositions that reflected
not just his own character," wrote Barbara Dafoe
Whitehead in an essay entitled *Franklin's Way to
Wealth*, "but the American character itself: the passion for freedom, the aspiration for self-improve-
ment, the pragmatic approach to problems, the
desire to do good, and the confident outlook on
the future."

Franklin was born January 17, 1706, the fif-
teenth of seventeen children. Due to limitations on
family finances, he was mostly self-educated. Even
though he had little formal education, he became

known as an intellectual, a literary genius, and a statesman in both Europe and America. Among the many honors bestowed on him, Franklin received honorary degrees from Yale, Harvard, William and Mary, Oxford, and St. Andrews. Because of his many important inventions and scientific discoveries, he was often labeled "the Newton of his age."

Franklin's bona fides as a Founding Father are confirmed by his signature on four major foundational documents including the Declaration of Independence, the Treaty of Alliance with France, the Treaty of Paris officially ending the Revolutionary War, and the U.S. Constitution. He was one of only six signers of the Declaration of Independence who also signed the Constitution.

The foundation for Franklin's impressive lifetime accomplishments, especially his extensive writings, was laid when he was a twelve-year-old printer's apprentice under his brother James, owner of the *New England Courant*. During his five years there, he began to write under the byline "Silence Dogood." His best-known and most enduring writing began in 1732 with the advent of his *Poor Richard's Almanack*, much of which is still in print today. A kind of secular book of proverbs, the *Almanack*, described by Franklin as "the wisdom of many ages and nations," eventually became second only to the Bible in popularity.

While his writings were infrequently couched in biblical terminology, the principles he advocated could often be traced to the Bible. For instance, this exhortation from *Poor Richard's Almanack*, which deals with slothfulness, a human trait disparaged in scripture, states: "He that riseth late, must trot all day, and shall scarce overtake his business at night."

On the subject of fools, a topic often addressed in the book of Proverbs, Franklin said, "Half Wits talk much but say little." "Tricks and treachery," he also wrote, "are the practice of fools that have not wit enough to be honest." Franklin observed an all-too-prevalent characteristic of modern man when he said, "Good Sense is a Thing all need, few have, and none think they want."

Regarding the biblical principle of forgiveness, Franklin advised, "Doing an Injury puts you below your Enemy; Revenging one makes you but even with him; Forgiving it sets you above him."

From all indications, Franklin tried to practice what he preached. From his autobiography, we know he carried with him a small book in which he had listed thirteen virtues; he made it a habit to concentrate on one specific virtue every day:

1. *Temperance: Eat not to dullness, drink not to elevation.*

2. *Silence: Speak not but what may benefit others or yourself; avoid trifling conversation.*

3. *Order: Let all your things have their places; let each part of business have its time.*

4. *Resolution: Resolve to perform what you ought; perform without fail what you resolve.*

5. *Frugality: Make no expense but to do good to others or yourself; i.e. waste nothing.*

6. *Industry: Lose no time; be always employ'd in something useful; cut off all unnecessary actions.*

7. *Sincerity: Use no hurtful deceit; think innocently and justly; and if you speak, speak accordingly.*

8. *Justice: Wrong none by doing injuries, or omitting the benefits that are your duty.*

9. *Moderation: Avoid extremes; forbear resenting injuries to much as you think they deserve.*

10. *Cleanliness: Tolerate no uncleanliness in body, cloaths, or habitations.*

11. *Tranquility: Be not disturbed at trifles, or at accidents common or unavoidable.*

12. *Chastity: Rarely use venery but for health or offspring, never to dullness, weakness, or the injury of your own or another's peace of reputation.*

13. *Humility: Imitate Jesus.*

Often referred to as a "Renaissance man," Franklin has been claimed by humanists as one of their own—because the period we know as the European Renaissance was characterized by a movement away from traditional spirituality. Franklin has also been called a deist by those who deny that he was Christian. According to *The New Oxford American Dictionary*, a deist is "a person who believes in the existence of a supreme being but one who does not interact with humankind." The "Franklin was a deist" claim may have been based on a pamphlet he wrote at the age of nineteen that he later tried to recall and destroy.

A deist would have had no inclination to call for prayer at the Constitutional Convention as Franklin did. "How has it happened," he asked, "that we have not hitherto once thought of humbly applying to the Father of lights to illuminate our understanding? In the beginning of the contest with Great Britain, when we were sensible of danger, we had daily prayer in this room for the Divine protection. Our prayers, Sir, were heard and they were graciously answered. All who were engaged in the struggle must have observed frequent instances of a superintending Providence in our favor. To that kind Providence, we owe this happy opportunity of consulting in peace on the means of establishing our future national felicity. And have we now forgotten this powerful Friend? Or do we imagine we no longer need His assistance?"

Regarding his personal religious beliefs, it is best to let Franklin speak for himself—as he did one month before he died at age eighty-five. In a letter to his friend Ezra Stiles, president of Yale College, he wrote: "You desire to know something of my Religion. It is the first time I have been questioned upon it: But I do not take your Curiosity amiss, and shall endeavour in a few Words to gratify it. Here is my Creed: I believe in one God, Creator of the Universe. That He governs it by his Providence. That he ought to be worshipped. That the most acceptable Service we can render to him is doing Good to his other Children. As to Jesus of Nazareth, my Opinion of whom you particularly desire, I think the System of Morals and his Religion as he left them to us, the best the World ever saw, or is likely to see; but I apprehend it has received various corrupting Changes, and I have with most of the present Dissenters in England, some Doubts as to his Divinity: tho' it is a Question I do not dogmatise upon, having never studied it, and think it needless to busy myself with it now, when I expect soon an Opportunity of knowing the Truth with less Trouble. I see no harm however in its being believed, if that Belief has the good Consequence as probably it has, of making his Doctrines more respected and better observed, especially as I do not perceive that the Supreme takes it amiss, by distinguishing the Believers, in his Government of the World, with any particular Marks of his Displeasure. I shall only add respecting myself, that having experienced the Goodness of that Being, in conducting me prosperously thro' a long Life, I have no doubt of its Continuance in the next, tho' without the smallest Conceit of meriting such Goodness."

Few knowledgeable historians deny that Franklin was a student of the Bible. When Franklin's friend Thomas Paine asked him for his thoughts prior to publication of Paine's controversial book *Age of Reason*, Franklin advised him in no uncertain terms to abandon the idea because of its anti-religion tone. In his response to Paine, Franklin wrote:

> *I have read your manuscript with some attention. By the argument it contains against a particular Providence, though you allow a general Providence, you strike at the foundations of all religion.* For without the belief of a Providence that takes cognizance of, guards, and guides, and may favor particular persons, there is no motive to worship a Deity, to fear his displeasure, or to pray for his protection. *I will not enter into any discussion of your principles though you seem to desire it. At present I shall only give you my opinion*

that. . .the consequence of printing this piece will be a great deal of odium drawn upon yourself, mischief to you and no benefit to others. He that spits into the wind, spits in his own face. But were you to succeed, do not imagine any good would be done by it. . . . [T]hink how great a portion of mankind consists of weak and ignorant men and women and of inexperienced, inconsiderate youth of both sexes who have need of the motives of religion to restrain them from vice, to support their virtue. . . . I would advise you, therefore, not to attempt unchaining the tiger, but to burn this piece before it is seen by any other person. . . . If men are so wicked with religion, what would they be if without it. *I intend this letter itself as a proof of my friendship.* (Emphasis added)

The Franklin family had their own designated pew in Philadelphia's Christ Church, which was located on the grounds in which the bodies of Franklin and seven other signers of the Declaration of Independence are interred. A plaque on that pew records the following historical fact: "Here worshipped Benjamin Franklin, philosopher and patriot and a Member of the Committee which erected the Spire of the Church. Interred according to the terms of his will in this churchyard."

In his *Articles of Belief and Acts of Religion*, Franklin wrote this prayer:

> *O Creator, O Father, I believe that Thou are Good, and Thou art pleas'd with the pleasure of Thy children. Praised be Thy Name forever.*
>
> *By Thy Power hast thou made the glorious Sun, with his attending worlds; from the energy of Thy mighty Will they first received their prodigious motion, and by Thy Wisdom hast Thou prescribed the wondrous laws by which they move. Praised be Thy Name forever.*
>
> *Thy Wisdom, Thy Power, and Thy GOODNESS are every where clearly seen; in the air and in the water, in the heavens and on the earth; Thou providest for the various winged fowl, and the innumerable inhabitants of the water; Thou givest cold and heat, rain and sunshine in their season, and to the fruits of the earth increase. Praised be Thy Name forever.*
>
> *Thou abhorrest in Thy creatures treachery and deceit, malice, revenge, intemperance and every other hurtful Vice; but Thou art a Lover of justice and*

sincerity, of friendship, benevolence and
every virtue. Thou art my Friend, my
Father, and my Benefactor. Praised be
Thy Name, O God, forever. Amen.

Franklin's epitaph, which he wrote himself at the age of twenty-two but was not engraved on his tombstone, said, "The body of B. Franklin, printer, like the cover of an old book, its contents worn out, and stript of its lettering and gilding, lies here, food for worms. Yet the work shall not be lost; for it will as he believ'd appear once more, in a new & more beautiful edition, corrected and amended by the Author."

Was Benjamin Franklin a Bible-believing Christian? His own words give us reason to hope he was.

Chapter Twelve

Noah Webster

Schoolmaster of the Nation

*The moral principles and precepts contained
in the Scriptures ought to form the basis of
all our civil constitutions and laws. All the
miseries and evils which men suffer from
vice, crime, ambition, injustice, oppression,
slavery, and war, proceed from their
despising or neglecting the precepts
contained in the Bible.*
NOAH WEBSTER

Although Noah Webster was a few months short
of his eighteenth birthday when the Declaration of
Independence was signed, he is usually included
among those known as Founding Fathers.

Webster took an active role in promoting ratification of the Constitution, even though he was

not a delegate to the Convention that produced it. Webster's pamphlets *Examination of the Leading Principles of the Federal Constitution* and *Sketches of American Policy* are credited with generating vital support for ratification.

He is primarily remembered as "the Schoolmaster of the Nation," a title he earned as the most active of the Founding Fathers in emphasizing the importance of an educated populace. Webster, who was known among his peers as a superior scholar and committed Christian, advocated government funding of education because he believed it was a responsibility of state and local governments to "discipline our youth in early life in sound maxims of moral, political, and religious duties."

In describing Webster's approach to education, H. R. Warfel, author of *Noah Webster: Schoolmaster to America*, wrote:

> *Along with good habits of work, Webster wished students to acquire "good principles, a predisposition for a virtuous life. For this reason society requires that the education of youth should be watched with the most scrupulous attention. Education, in a great measure, forms the moral character of men, and morals are the basis of government. Education should therefore be the first care of a legislature;*

not merely the institution of schools, but the furnishing of them with the best men for teachers. A good system of education should be the first article in the code of political regulations; for it is much easier to introduce and establish an effectual system for preserving morals, than to correct by penal statues the ill effects of a bad system." On this point Webster was emphatic; he asserted: "The goodness of a heart is of infinitely more consequence to society than an elegance of manners; nor will any superficial accomplishments repair the want of principle in the mind. It is always better to be vulgarly right than politely wrong. The education of youth [is] an employment of more consequence than making laws and preaching the gospel, because it lays the foundation on which both law and gospel rest for success."

Webster's first contribution to the field of elementary education was his *American Spelling Book,* which was published in 1783 and included "an easy Standard of Pronunciation." Commonly known as "the blue-backed speller," it eventually became an all-time bestseller with more than 70 million copies sold. His pronunciation guide later became part of *A Grammatical Institute of the*

English Language.

"Noah Webster's Speller," explained Verna Hall, author of *The Christian History of the Constitution of the United States of America,* "was compatible with the hearthside of a log cabin in the wilderness, or a city classroom. It traveled on the flatboats of the Ohio River, churned down the Mississippi and creaked across the prairies of the far west as pioneer mothers taught their children from covered wagons. Wherever the individual wished to challenge his own ignorance or quench his thirst for knowledge, there, along with the Holy Bible and Shakespeare, were Noah Webster's slim and inexpensive Spellers, Grammars, Readers and his *Elements of Useful Knowledge* containing the history and geography of the United States. Webster's books were unlike texts seen today, for they openly presented biblical admonitions, as well as principles of American government. In one of his early editions of the 'blue-backed speller' appeared a 'Moral Catechism'—rules upon which to base moral conduct. Webster stated unequivocally, 'God's Word, contained in the Bible, has furnished all necessary rules to direct our conduct.'"

Words were a passion, language an obsession with Webster. At the age of fourteen, he began studying classic literature with the Reverend Nathan Perkins as his tutor. Two years later, he enrolled at Yale College, where he gravitated toward lexicography and philology. After leaving Yale, Webster studied law in his spare time and was admitted to the bar in 1781.

In his *Rudiments of English Grammar*, published in 1790, Webster continued his campaign to draw lines of distinction between the American version of the English language and the established British version. He was influential in the difficult task of clarifying many of the differences that had evolved in the colonies in the way the language was spoken, words were spelled and pronounced, and in the rules of grammar.

Between 1806 and 1833, Webster produced, among other writings, *A Compendious Dictionary of the English Language*; *A Philosophical and Practical Grammar of the English Language*; *A Synopsis of Words in Twenty Languages*; *The American Dictionary*; *An American Dictionary of the English Language—with pronouncing vocabularies of Scripture, classical and geographical names*, and his *History of the United States*. He also produced a Bible translation entitled *Common Version of the Holy Bible, containing the Old and New Testament, with Amendments of the Language*. In 1840, an expanded edition of his 1828 dictionary, containing more than 70,000 words, was published.

In the preface of each of his books, Webster included comments explaining his belief that the Christian religion and the Bible were the bedrocks of American civilization and the only safeguards against tyranny. This statement appearing in the preface of his Bible translation is typical of all of his book introductions:

> *The Bible is the Chief moral cause of all that is good, and the best corrector of all that is evil, in human society; the best book for regulating the temporal concerns of men, and the only book that can serve as an infallible guide to future felicity. It is extremely important to our nation, in a political as well as religious view, that all possible authority and influence should be given to the scriptures, for these furnish the best principles of civil liberty, and the most effectual support of republican government.*
>
> *The principles of genuine liberty, and of wise laws and administrations, are to be drawn from the Bible and sustained by its authority. The man, therefore, who weakens or destroys the divine authority of that Book, may be accessory to all the public disorders which society is doomed to suffer.*
>
> *There are two powers only, sufficient to control men and secure the rights of individuals and a peaceable*

*administration; these are the combined
force of religion and law, and the force or
fear of the bayonet.*

Webster included *Advice to the Young* in his *Value
of the Bible and Excellence of the Christian Religion*, which he wrote as a companion piece to his
translation of the King James Bible. His advice is as
timely and valuable today as it was in 1833:

*When you become entitled to exercise
the right of voting for public officers, let
it be impressed on your mind that God
commands you to choose for rulers, just
men who will rule in the fear of God. The
preservation of a republican government
depends on the faithful discharge of this
duty; if the citizens neglect their duty,
and place unprincipled men in office,
the government will soon be corrupted;
laws will be made, not for the public
good, so much as for selfish or local
purposes; corrupt or incompetent men
will be appointed to execute the laws;
the public revenues will be squandered
on unworthy men; and the rights of the
citizens will be violated or disregarded. If
a republican government fails to secure
public prosperity and happiness, it must*

be because the citizens neglect the divine commands, and elect bad men to make and administer the laws. Intriguing men can never be safely trusted. . . .

The most perfect maxims and examples for regulating your social conduct and domestic economy, as well as the best rules of morality and religion, are to be found in the Bible. The history of the Jews presents the true character of man in all its forms. All the traits of human character, good and bad, all the passions of the human heart; all the principles which guide and misguide men in society, are depicted in that short history, with an artless simplicity that has no parallel in modern writings. As to maxims of wisdom or prudence, the Proverbs of Solomon furnish a complete system, and sufficient, if carefully observed, to make any man wise, prosperous, and happy. The observation that "a soft answer turneth away wrath," if strictly observed by men, would prevent half the broils and contentions that inflict wretchedness on society and families. . . . All the miseries and evils which men suffer from vice, crime, ambition, injustice, oppression, slavery, and war, proceed from their

*despising or neglecting the precepts
contained in the Bible.*

*As the means of temporal happiness
then the Christian religion ought to be
received, and maintained with firm and
cordial support. It is the real source of all
genuine republican principles. It teaches
the equality of men as to rights and
duties; and while it forbids all oppression,
it commands due subordination to law
and rulers. It requires the young to yield
obedience to their parents, and enjoins
upon men the duty and wisdom, and
real religion—"men who fear God and
hate covetousness." The ecclesiastical
establishments of Europe, which serve
to support tyrannical governments, are
not the Christian religion, but abuses
and corruptions of it. The religion of
Christ and his apostles, in its primitive
simplicity and purity, unencumbered
with the trappings of power and the
pomp of ceremonies is the surest basis of a
republican government. . . .*

*For instruction then in social, religious,
and civil duties, resort to the scriptures
for the best precepts and most excellent
examples for imitation. The example
of unhesitating faith and obedience in*

Abraham, when he promptly prepared to offer his son Isaac, as a burnt offering, at the command of God, is a perfect model of that trust in God which becomes dependent beings. The history of Joseph furnishes one of the most charming examples of fraternal affection, and of filial duty and respect for a venerable father, ever exhibited in human life. Christ and his apostles presented, in their lives, the most perfect example of disinterested benevolence, unaffected kindness, humility, patience in adversity, forgiveness of injuries, love to God, and to all mankind. If men would universally cultivate these religious affections and virtuous dispositions, with as much diligence as they cultivate human science and refinement of manners, the world would soon become a terrestrial paradise.

Webster's description of his conversion to the Christian faith should serve as an important example and warning to young people today:

Being educated in a religious family under pious parents, I had in early life some religious impressions, but being too young to understand fully the

doctrines of the Christian religion, and
falling into vicious company at college,
I lost those impressions. [I] fell into the
common mistake of attending to the
duties which man owes to man before
I had learned the duties which we all
owe to our Creator and Redeemer. I
sheltered myself as well as I could from
the attacks of conscience for neglect of
duty under a species of skepticism, and
endeavored to satisfy my mind that a
profession of religion is not absolutely
necessary to salvation. In this state of
mind I placed great reliance on good
works or the performance of moral duties
as the means of salvation. About a year
ago, an unusual revival of religion took
place in New Haven. and [I] was led by
a spontaneous impulse to repentance,
prayer, and entire submission and
surrender of myself to my Maker and
Redeemer. I now began to understand
and relish many parts of the Scriptures
which before appeared mysterious and
unintelligible, or repugnant to my nature.
In short, my view of the Scriptures, of
religion, of the whole Christian scheme of
salvation, and of God's moral government
are very much changed, and my heart

> *yields with delight and confidence to*
> *whatever appears to be the Divine will.*

Born in Hartford, Connecticut, October 16, 1758, Webster, on his father's side, was a fourth-generation descendant of John Webster, one of the first settlers of Hartford, and, on his mother's side, a descendant of William Bradford, a passenger on the Mayflower. Bradford, who was elected governor of Plymouth Colony thirty times, also organized the first Thanksgiving Day celebration in New England.

In addition to his unmatched contributions to the nation's emerging Bible-based system of education, Webster's résumé included the following: Member of the American Philosophical Society in Philadelphia; Fellow of the American Academy of Arts and Sciences in Massachusetts; Member of the Connecticut Academy of Arts and Sciences; Fellow of the Royal Society of Northern Antiquaries in Copenhagen; Member of the Connecticut Historical Antiquaries in Copenhagen; Member of the Connecticut Historical Society; Corresponding Member of the Historical Societies in Massachusetts, New York, and Georgia; the Academy of Medicine in Philadelphia; the Columbian Institute in Washington; and Honorary Member of the Michigan Historical Society. He also served as a soldier in the Revolutionary War.

Webster died May 28, 1843, in New Haven.

In his "Memoir of the Author," the editor of *The American Dictionary*, concluded:

> *It may be said that the name Noah Webster, from the wide circulation of some of his works, is known familiarly to a greater number of the inhabitants of the United States, than the name, probably, of any other individual except the father of the Country. Whatever influence he thus acquired was used at all time to promote the best interests of his fellow men. His books, though read by millions, have made no man worse. To multitudes they have been of lasting benefit not by the course of early training they have furnished, but by those precepts of wisdom and virtue with which almost every page is stored. August, 1847.*

Like his fellow Founding Fathers, Noah Webster was a dedicated patriot. These stirring words of his need to be remembered today when patriotism is sometimes mocked: "Our fathers were men—they were heroes and patriots—they fought—they conquered—and they bequeathed to us a rich inheritance of liberty and empire which we have no right to surrender. Yes, my fellow freemen, we have a rich and growing empire—we have a lucrative commerce to protect—we have indefeasible rights—we have an excellent system of religion and of government—we have wives and children and sisters to defend; and God forbid that the soil of America should sustain the wretch who [lacks] the will or the spirit to defend them. Let us then rally round the independence and Constitution of our country, resolved to a man that we will never lose by folly, disunion, or cowardice what has been planned by wisdom and purchased with blood."

Epilogue

*A wholesome regard for the memory of the
great men of long ago is the best assurance
to a people of a continuation of great men to
come who shall be able to instruct, to lead,
and to inspire. A people who worship at
the shrine of true greatness will
themselves be truly great.*
CALVIN COOLIDGE

A not-to-be denied desire to live free was a common attribute among the unusually courageous, determined, and adventuresome individuals who traveled across dangerous waters, journeying thousands of miles in primitive ships, to reach the shores of the New World. Those same characteristics were common among America's Founding Fathers, who originated our unique systems of government and commerce based on biblical precepts of freedom, personal responsibility, and accountability to the one true God. Exceptional men and women discovered, settled, and established the United States of America.

Edward Everett (1794–1865) wrote this excellent tribute to our Founders:

SUCH MEN CANNOT DIE

No, fellow-citizens, we dismiss not Adams and Jefferson to the chambers of forgetfulness and death. What we admired, and prized, and venerated in them, can never die, nor, dying, be forgotten. I had almost said that they are now beginning to live—to live that life of unimpaired influence, of unclouded fame, of unmingled happiness, for which their talents and services were destined. They were of the select few, the least portion of whose life dwells in their physical existence; whose hearts have watched while their senses slept; whose souls have grown up into a higher being; whose pleasure is to be useful; whose wealth is an unblemished reputation; who respire the breath of honorable fame; who have deliberately and consciously put what is called life to hazard, that they may live in the hearts of those who come after. Such men do not, can not die.

To be cold, and motionless, and breathless, to feel not and speak not: this is not the end of existence to the men who have breathed their spirits into the institutions of their country, who have stamped their characters on the pillars of the age, who have poured their hearts' blood into the channels of the public prosperity. . . . Tell me, ye who make your pious pilgrimage to the shades of Vernon, is Washington indeed shut up in that old and narrow house? That which made these men, and men like these, cannot die. The hand that traced the charter of independence is, indeed, motionless, the eloquent lips that sustained it are hushed; but the lofty spirits that conceived, resolved, matured, maintained it, and which alone, to such men, "make it life to live," these cannot expire:

> *These shall resist the empire of decay,*
> *When time is o'er, and worlds have*
> *passed away:*
> *Cold in the dust the perished heart*
> *may lie,*
> *But that which warmed it once can*
> *never die.*

We should continue to find inspiration in the wisdom and character of the people who, relying upon the precepts of the Bible, designed a government that has provided more freedom, more opportunities, and a higher quality of life for its citizens than any other nation in history. Making certain that our children and grandchildren understand their history and their godly heritage is one of the most important gifts we can give them.

They need to know that America's Founding Fathers were inspired and motivated by Psalm 33:12: "Blessed is the nation whose God is the Lord."

Share the wonder
of American history
with the children
in your life

Help your kids understand our national experience with *Kids' Guide to American History*. This fully-illustrated guide for 8-to-12 year olds explains US history from a Christian perspective! Describing the who, what, when, where, and why of American history, it covers eight major periods—pre-colonial; colonial; birth of the United States; national growth and challenges (Louisiana Purchase through the Compromise of 1850); slavery and Civil War; industrialization, economic growth, and immigration (late 1800s through World War I); America as world power (World War II through the end of Cold War); and the 21st century. Intriguing trivia adds to the fun, and it's all wrapped up in a bright, colorful package that kids will love.

ISBN 978-1-61626-600-4 / Paperback
160 pages / 7.5" x 9.5"

Available wherever Christian books are sold.